From Spare Room to Sp _____

TURNING YOUR EXTRA SPACE INTO AN AIRBNB

Crystal Rusteen

This guide is written from a combination of experience and high-level research. Even though we have done our best to ensure this book is accurate and up to date, there are no guarantees to the accuracy or completeness of the contents herein.

This book has been designed using resources from unsplash.com and www.pexels.com.
ISBN: 978-1-953714-44-2

REVIEWS

Reviews and feedback help improve this book and the author. If you enjoy this book, we would greatly appreciate it if you could take a few moments to share your opinion and post a review on Amazon.

CONTENTS

INTRODUCTION

Some say it's the way we'll all travel in the future. Others feel that the concept is reminiscent of how we made our way from town to town in the past. Either way, it seems very clear that the idea of Airbnbs isn't going anywhere any time soon.

In fact, there's merit to both claims. Many applaud Airbnb's mission to change the way we travel. If more people invite travelers into their homes, that cuts back on the expenses and environmental impact of enormous hotels. Additionally, it creates warm, welcoming spaces and experiences for those who might otherwise find themselves disconnected from their destinations. And for some, it's a fantastic opportunity to make a little money without making a huge sacrifice.

It's also true that in the not-so-distant past, many weary travelers relied upon the hospitality of strangers as they walked from one location to the next. Hostels, inns and taverns were not only places to get a hot meal and rest easy for the night, but were also homes to the families that ran those businesses.

The idea of opening up your home to others for a few nights is definitely not a new concept, but our modern world has changed many aspects of how we procure a place to stay for the night. For example, instead of walking, riding a horse, or taking a carriage from one location to another, we typically hop in the car, take a train, or book a flight. Once we arrive, some of us stick around for a few nights, visiting with loved ones or checking out the local sights. On the other hand, some travelers like to have a quick getaway to a nearby location for a little change of scenery or a night out on the town.

We also have the internet, which has not only made the process of finding a place to stay easier than ever but has taken some of the mystery out of what to expect once we arrive. Instead of relying on word of mouth or a single picture in the back of a travel magazine, we can scroll through many different reviews, recommendations, and photos of the interior and exterior of any place we might choose to stay. This level of transparency can help us feel safer and more secure in knowing that we're not going to end up in a Bates Motel-type situation or have to share the room with a family of cockroaches.

Airbnb allows individuals to open up their homes to a variety of guests while connecting guests with comfortable and reliable living spaces for the duration of their trip. At the time of publishing, there are quite a few different companies around the world or at the regional level that are helping connect travelers with a place to stay. Since some of these are more localized, it would be impossible to name them all, especially with the rapidly changing travel scene. For the most part, the tips, ideas, and recommendations presented in this book will apply to any temporary home rental company, but bear in mind that exact policies and requirements may differ from business to business.

As a traveler, you may have experienced an Airbnb yourself. There are plenty of draws to the concept, and you may have found yourself falling in love with any part of the process. Perhaps, as you were scrolling through ads or packing up to check out of an Airbnb, you thought to yourself, "this would be a fun little side-hustle." Or maybe you've got a fantastic home in a great location that you'd love to share with others. If for any reason you've thought about the many benefits of becoming an Airbnb host, then this book is for you.

Like nearly every new endeavor, there will be a lot of ideas that you've already stashed away for your "maybe someday" Airbnb, but there are likely quite a few things you haven't yet considered. That's normal. The purpose of this book is to help open your eyes to things you may not have considered and to clarify any points that you might only vaguely understand.

We'll start by looking at the practicality of turning your home into an Airbnb. There are tons of different types of housing arrangements offered on the site, from a spare bedroom in a family home, to houses suspended from trees in the middle of absolutely nowhere. Just as there isn't one type of traveler, there isn't just one type of Airbnb property, which is why so many people have the opportunity to become hosts. Having a great place to spend the night is just the tip of the iceberg. We'll explore all of the different things you need to take into account when it comes to deciding whether to list your house.

Afterwards, we'll move into the process of creating the overall ambiance for your place. After all, this is your property we're talking about– from the furnishings to the extra touches; you'll need to be on top of every detail. Since you'll be in charge of your guests' experience, you want to provide the perfect setting in whatever way translates to your overall vision for their stay. From rustic to eclectic, from luxe to unique, you may have trouble in narrowing down your vision to an actual plan. There are so many different aesthetics and concepts you can pursue, all of which have plenty of draw to those looking for an ideal place to stay. We'll take you through all the steps you'll need to bear in mind, along with tips and tricks to help you make each stay truly special.

Next, we'll take a look at some of the easiest ways to communicate rules. Boundaries are crucial when welcoming strangers into your home, regardless of whether you'll be there during the stay or not. Providing a house manual and detailed information about check-in can help make the process of coming and going easy for your guests, while establishing clear rules will make sure everyone has a pleasant stay. Communication is key, so you'll want to be prepared to share information that will keep everyone safe and comfortable.

We'll look at what happens when established rules aren't followed, or when things go wrong unexpectedly. There are times when whatever can possibly go wrong will go wrong, which generally creates a domino effect of disaster. While it's impossible to completely prevent bad things from happening, you can be armed with the knowledge and forethought to take care of these incidents before a small problem escalates into a tragedy.

Once we've covered the groundwork for establishing your Airbnb, from creating an experience to dealing with the unexpected, we'll assemble the major concepts into a comprehensive checklist, along with a detailed "pros and cons" list to help you feel confident with your final decision. So, will you take the plunge and become a top-rated Airbnb host, or do you need more time to figure out the logistics?

While we can't answer this question for you, if you decide you're ready, we want you to be as well prepared as possible and get the most out of being a host.

SECTION 1:
SHOULD YOU MAKE YOUR HOME AN AIRBNB?

The idea of becoming a successful Airbnb host may be very appealing in theory, but how does the process play out in reality? Whether you're interested in creating a lodging empire through your endeavors or just hope to make a little extra money while helping people out, there are a lot of considerations that lie between contemplating the possibility and making it happen.

In an ideal world, people could come and go as they pleased, with no more risk to the host than muddy footprints in the foyer. But that's not how the real world works.

Before you even start daydreaming about opening your home to others, you need to understand what you're getting into. Perhaps you love sharing your home with guests,getting your home ready for weekend visitors really energizes you, and you appreciate every opportunity to entertain others and introduce them to your hometown. Maybe you have an absolutely exquisite home that you love sharing with others. You may own a home in a very desirable neighborhood or a home in an exotic location where finding people eager for "any ol' place to stay" can make you a bundle of money. You might find yourself with an extra property or two, with no practical plans for them– so why not let them generate some extra income?

But before you hop online and start drafting your listing, it's important to consider what the experience is really going to be like. While you may have had plenty of luck opening your home to familiar guests in the past, this is going to be an entirely different enterprise. These travelers do not know you. They may not be familiar with the area in which you live. They may come from a different background and have expectations that do not align with the services you provide.

It's important to stop and consider all of the logistics before posting your home online. There are many moving pieces that keep an Airbnb operating like a well-oiled machine. First, you need to figure out the logistics, such as why someone would want to stay at your place as well as recognizing and accommodating their needs. What are your goals? What do you hope to get out of this experience, and what kind of experience do you hope to provide. There's so much more to the process than putting clean sheets on the bed and setting a price.

There is a place for absolutely every home on Airbnb, but the question is: will people think their experience is worth it? And, perhaps even more importantly, will *you* find the whole experience worth it in the end?

Chapter 1: About Your Home

There are likely many things you love about your home. After all, there are millions of factors that go into turning a house into a home. What do you consider the best features of your home? Is it how the decor perfectly reflects your personality? Is it the furniture that you sink into at the end of a long day? Maybe it's a convenient location near all of your neighborhood haunts. Or, quite the opposite, the fact that there are no neighbors for miles and miles.

Everyone is drawn to a particular dwelling, whether it's a unique conversion in the woods or a stately downtown apartment. The opposite is true, as well. Some people would go to great lengths to never set foot in a tent, while others would rather do anything else than find parallel parking on crowded city street.

All of this may seem like common sense, so why mention it? When it comes to establishing your own Airbnb experience, you need to understand the specific draw of your home. While you and your friends may love and appreciate your home, it's time to step back and look at it objectively. If you had never seen your house before, would you be excited to stay there? What circumstances would lead you to want or need to stay there? What do you have to offer that's different from any other home in the area?

Not every Airbnb is born out of the desire for a unique experience. Some of the listings are clearly strategic postings for weary travelers who are only looking for a comfortable place to land for the night. These Airbnbs can be especially helpful in more rural areas, where finding a hotel room may require hours of driving or more money than the average budget would allow.

The first step to opening your home as an Airbnb is to understand where your home fits into the grand scheme of things. One helpful exercise is to go straight to the source and see what's available in your area.

Head to Airbnb (or multiple sites for a greater perspective) and start searching in your immediate area. Then expand your search. Go into the neighboring counties and look at the various opportunities across your state.

You'll likely notice there are a variety of different lodging options available. For example, some properties can offer you a private room only. That means that anyone staying at that property will likely share the house or apartment with other residents, but they're paying for a private bed. These arrangements are usually the least expensive, and for a good reason. There are often few amenities or luxury touches, and less privacy.

Some listings promise an entire suite. These suites generally include a bedroom and bathroom, and in some cases, a private entrance or sitting room. Of course, the person renting the suite for the night will still be in close proximity to the residents, but there are certain advantages to shelling out extra money for an entire suite. For example, they won't have to wait for the bathroom to be open, and may be able to come and go as they please.

Other properties are entirely available to the renter, whether they take the form of an entire apartment, an entire house, or more experience-driven homes such as cabins, tents, yurts, and tiny homes. In this case, the individual or group that rents the property will have the whole space to themselves, including living areas, kitchen, bedroom(s), and bathroom(s).

Some properties don't fit exactly into these molds. One of Airbnb's greatest draws is the impressive selection of unique dwellings, from houses high in the treetops to fascinating conversions that turn a strange setting into a hospitable place to spend a night. You can also find desirable camping spaces, or if "glamping" is more your style, many camper trailers and RVs owners are opening up their spaces to travelers, With the more outdoorsy arrangements, you may not have a dedicated bathroom or shampoo waiting for you in the shower, but you will have a memorable stay.

So, with all these options in mind, where does your home fit in the equation?

Let's start by evaluating your living situation. Are you planning to rent a room, your entire home, or a specific property you plan to dedicate to renting, such as a vacation home, camping spot, or RV?

People want to rent an Airbnb based on location, practicality, cost, and desired experience. In which of these areas does your home truly excel? What are some things that might be challenging when opening up your home to others? You can overcome many challenges through honesty and a little troubleshooting, but it's important to be aware of these realities so that you can set up accurate expectations for your guests.

Objectively speaking, how would you describe your space? Is it a three-bedroom house, a flexible loft, an isolated cabin, or a metropolitan guest suite? Think in terms of what your home has to offer inside. How many people can comfortably sleep there? Would it be practical to allow guests to set up air mattresses, cribs, or sleeping bags? These types of considerations can make a huge difference for travelers, and it's something to think about before you create your listing.

As you're considering the interior, think about what happens outside, as well. What's the parking situation like? What's the neighborhood like? What expectations do your neighbors have? Are there any attractions, restaurants, or fun gathering places nearby, and if so, are they close enough to walk? Are there rideshare opportunities available? These are things that will matter to many travelers. A 30-minute drive to the nearest grocery store is a very different experience than a 3-minute walk to the local market, and these aspects will make a difference to your potential guests.

As you're considering these factors, try to envision the type of person who would appreciate your space the most. Your honesty is going to be helpful for every future traveler who considers your Airbnb. If you live in a building where music is always playing, food is always cooking, and the neighbors are always shouting at each other in the hallways, you'll have a hard time attracting travelers who are looking for a quiet, isolated, romantic weekend. If your prospective Airbnb property is a cabin deep in the woods, far from any trace of a cell phone signal, it's crucial your guests don't expect 24-hour grocery delivery at the click of a button. Likewise, having several flights of stairs, detached bathrooms, or multiple people sharing a bathroom is worth noting. In addition, proximity to resources like groceries, hospitals, or police are the types of details that your future bookers will seriously consider before paying to stay in your home.

Your house is far more than the comfort of your bed linens or the view you have of the sunrise. All of the quirks of your home, your neighborhood, even your city, town, or municipality, can impact the overall experience your visitors have at your home.

Another thing to bear in mind is that your guests may perceive your home in a totally different light. Their experiences and preferences will guide their opinions. Perhaps the parking situation you see as "no-hassle" might be a massive inconvenience to someone else, or your "stunning view" might be underwhelming to someone with different expectations. It's important to note that not every guest will be 100% satisfied with every aspect of their stay. Just as two people in the same room can debate whether it's too hot or too cold, your guests may not love your space as much as you do. However, portraying your place as honestly and prac-tically as you can – first to yourself and then in your Airbnb listing – will be the gateway to creating the best possible experience for your guests.

When beginning the process of listing your home as an Airbnb, you need to set realistic expectations about the experience. If you own a great house, but the basement bedroom you're thinking of renting floods when it rains, this may not be the best choice. If your apartment is central to all the cool things to do in your city, but there's nowhere to park or even pull up a car to drop off luggage, you might want to take a hard look at your potential success as a host.

Remember, your house doesn't have to be ready *this very instant*, and there's always room to grow as you funnel your extra income into improving your home. But if you look around and realize there are more obstacles than you're prepared to take on right now, perhaps it's time to set aside your Airbnb goals today and look forward to building towards that dream at a future date.

Ultimately, as long as your home is clean and in good repair, it is appropriate for listing on Airbnb. First, however, you will want to take stock of all of your home's features, both individually and on the whole, to ensure that you can provide your guests with a desirable and enjoyable experience. Go beyond the obvious reasons you love your home, and consider what it can provide to anyone. From a place to hang your hat for the night, to a unique experience offered by no other home in the world, there are plenty of folks willing to pay for the privilege of sleeping in your house, and now you're getting closer to making that a possibility.

Chapter 2: Is It Feasible?

Once you've taken stock of your home and location, it's time to think about the realities of renting out your home to complete strangers.

This decision likely requires more thought than you might expect at first. You'll need to consider almost every aspect of your life, home, location, your time, and your money. While renting your space as an Airbnb can be financially lucrative, you'll still need to invest in your space and your vision to get started. Airbnb and other rental companies will have requirements you will have to factor into your initial investment, and the guests themselves will want or need amenities and extras that you will have to provide. Remember, these folks will be coming to live in your space temporarily, based only on a few pictures and an online description.

The following list identifies nine specific areas you should consider before taking the plunge into Airbnb hosting. Each step covers a fundamental aspect of the hosting and rental process. Make sure you carefully think about each so you can be completely confident that your home or extra space is ready to welcome guests from around the world.

1: Can Your Space Be Rented?

First things first: Make sure it's ok to rent out your space. Start at the local level of your town or city. Is renting your home legal? Are there any lease or deed restrictions that address how often you can rent out your home, or the circumstances under which you can host others for a temporary period? What are the consequences if you're caught violating these provisions? It's easy to take a "catch me if you can" attitude about rules and laws that you disagree with, but remember, Airbnb is a very public website. Next, make sure renting your space is permitted by your building, landlord, or Homeowner's Association. Again, you may be tempted to roll your eyes and disregard the regulations, but if your building or HOA has the power to evict you, you may want to play by their rules or take the opportunity to make a strong case for yourself in front of those in charge before you take matters into your own hands.

2: What about Other Household Members?

After all of the legalities have been sorted out, you next have to address the matter of the household occupants. If you're the only person who lives in the space you intend to rent, this will be a very short conversation. You simply need to decide whether you'll share the space with your renters or give them the entire place while you find somewhere else to go during their stay. If you're renting a property other than your primary residence, you don't necessarily need to make the decision of whether to stay or go; however, you will need to make sure you can be easily reached in case something goes wrong. Don't worry, we'll cover that topic in detail in a later chapter.

If you have a family, roommates, or others who utilize the space, you'll want to take into account their sentiments as well. Even if you live in an adjacent property or are renting out a distant vacation home, you'll want to make sure that everyone who could possibly be impacted fully understands the situation. For example, if your cousin has a key to your lakeside tiny house, you'll probably want to let him know that you plan on renting it out before he randomly walks in on a paying guest. Make sure that everyone who is involved with your household is on board with your decision. No one wants to be surprised by a complete stranger in their home, whether they're a visitor or a full-time resident. For the other occupants of your space, knowing about the comings and goings of Airbnb guests will give them time to make decisions regarding their own arrivals and departures.

3: Considering Your Lifestyle

The Airbnb application not only allows hosts to share pictures and descriptions of their property, but also allows hosts to set a calendar of availability for renters. Overall availability is essential for hosts to consider because it requires you to think about where you'll be while others are in your space. Planning out your availability also means you'll need to think about what's going on at your property at any given time.

For example, if you have a deluxe downtown condo that would be perfect for weekend getaways, but during the summers roads are often shut down for an entire day due to street festivals or events, you might want to prohibit folks from renting your space on those days. Unless they're in town specifically to participate in those events, they likely aren't going to appreciate being held hostage in your condo until the local authorities open up the streets again.

Are there times of the year when it might be less than ideal for strangers to attempt to navigate your neighborhood? From street festivals to annual garage sales and regular road maintenance, the activities that you may appreciate in your area might not be as fun for road-weary travelers trying to get around town for the first time. While you can't control these events, you can keep them in mind when permitting guest rentals.

Additionally, renting out your home while you spend two months abroad may seem like a great way to use your space while generating some passive income while you're away, but who will be your local point of contact if something goes awry? Who will you trust to inspect the property between visitors to ensure it's in tip-top shape, and if it's not, to make any adjustments needed?

Some individuals have a reliable place to stay if their own homes are rented out, but that doesn't mean it's always practical or convenient to crash there while your place is being rented. Think about your schedule carefully. If it would make more sense for you to stay in your own home during a certain time frame, don't attempt to bend time and space just to make a little extra money. The payoff is rarely so significant that it would make complicated, time-consuming, last minute plans worth the stress and agony. Plan wisely.

4: Pets and Other Companions

Considering the needs of your housemates extends to your furry, feathered, or finned friends, as well. How do your pets feel about guests? Do they travel well? Do you trust them around people they've never met and vice-versa? Can your pets be locked up safely if, for some reason, they do not take to your guests – or the other way around?

This consideration is particularly important if you're hosting a farm stay experience that includes livestock. Not only do you need to make guests aware of the multiple animals on-site, but you may have to specify the types of sounds, smells, and situations they may encounter during their stay. For example, if you have a herd of sheep and several working guard dogs, you may need to clarify that the dogs aren't cuddly, the sheep don't like being chased, and the fence is electrified. These may all seem like obvious points to you, but they may not be for someone who has never set foot on a farm.

Another issue is potential allergies. Cat and dog owners are well aware that hair, fur, and dander are everywhere. The very dust that wafts through your home is full of reminders that there are pets in the house. You will already need to clean and sanitize intensely to alleviate any potential allergy issues for guests, but it may be impossible to remove every trace of your pets' existence. Even these small traces of your pets can be a massive problem for guests with very sensitive allergies.

On the flip side, some Airbnb properties pride themselves on being pet-friendly, meaning guests are welcome to bring their well-behaved critters with them. Whether or not you implement a pet-friendly policy is an important decision to make. Obviously, pets bring with them the potential for accidents (potty-related or otherwise). Still, if you have a furry companion, you can understand why having a place that allows pets can be a huge bonus for many travelers.

Basically, you have two decisions to make: First, is it reasonable to rent your space as an Airbnb with your current pet situation, and second, do you want to welcome guest's pets into your home? Again, this is not a decision to be taken lightly, so be sure to give it serious thought.

Once you've got yourself, your family, your crew, and your pets all sorted. That should do the trick, right? Well, not exactly. Now it's time to think about the space itself and everything that exists within it, day in and day out.

5: Your Belongings

If you're planning to rent out a property that isn't your primary home, you'll have greater control over your belongings than other Airbnb arrangements. Generally speaking, you don't have a lot of valuable personal effects at a vacation home, camper, or rental property. Whatever you keep there can likely be moved to another location or secured from the view of any strangers.

But, if you're going to rent your main residence, you'll need to think carefully about all of your belongings. Sure, your sofa may not have been very expensive, but how much of a hassle would it be to replace it if something were to happen?

While most people who use Airbnb are kind and have no intention of making mischief, you have to consider the fact that, no matter how nice the person may seem, you are still renting out your space to strangers. Even the most conscientious guest can accidentally tip over a coffee. Therefore, when taking stock of your space, really think about how you would feel if any of your decorations were broken, stained, or otherwise damaged.

You will also have to accept that not every traveler will be as respectful of other peoples' property as you may prefer. While Airbnb has provisions in place to prevent scammers and weed out renters who may have a Motley Crue-level of interest in trashing the place, there are still circumstances that no one can possibly predict. While we'll get more in-depth regarding what could happen and what to do if it does later in this book, now is the time to gauge whether you are really and truly comfortable with the idea of just about anyone spending time unsupervised in your space.

There are measures you can take to mitigate the risks. For example, Airbnb highly recommends that you lock up everything and anything that has monetary or personal value to you. That way you have the opportunity to stage your space in a way that not only accommodates the needs of your guests, but prevents the loss of any of your favorite possessions. Again, we'll get into further detail on staging in the next section. However, this is a great time to brainstorm ways you can make your house "stranger proof." Perhaps you find a cover for your sofa and swap out your relatives' antiques for less meaningful decor from thrift shops or dollar stores. You don't want to create a clandestine, bare-bones experience for your guests, but you don't have to let them eat off your great-great-great grandmother's fine china either.

Your home may then feel like it takes on a sort of split reality. There's the home you live in, with the fine china and antique collection, and there's the place you rent out on Airbnb. Will you have time to switch back and forth easily between the two, or will it take you a few days to get things back to "normal?" Cleaning and staging your home for Airbnb guests can take a lot of time, and if time is not a resource you have in excess, you'll want to come up with a game plan for your space right away.

Remember, you have control over when your home is available. You can select check-in and check-out times that make sense for you and your schedule. However, if you find yourself spending more time staging and changing your home's decor to accommodate Airbnb guests than you do enjoying it, you might need to reevaluate your process.

6: Cleaning and Staging

Cleaning is another major factor of the Airbnb experience. Hosts are not required to have their homes professionally cleaned; however, following the COVID-19 pandemic of 2020-21, the site does ask hosts to adhere to a 5-step enhanced cleaning process. This process requires hosts to:

1. Prepare yourself and your space by ventilating the space and disinfecting your hands
2. Clean all surfaces, fixtures, laundry, and dishes
3. Sanitize with products recommended by your local health guidelines
4. Complete an online checklist
5. Reset all of the cleaned items and disinfect your cleaning products

Hosts are also asked to follow local health department guidelines and laws regarding the sanitation of shared or rented spaces.

Airbnb takes these practices very seriously. Hosts who commit to the 5-step enhanced cleaning process have a specific badge displayed on their listings to indicate to potential guests that the property is thoroughly sanitized and cleaned. For some, failure to comply may result in the company blocking your property from future reservations.

These policies and procedures may vary between other home-sharing and vacation rental companies, but regardless of which site you choose to host through, be sure to review all of the requirements for cleaning posted on their information pages or FAQs. Some sites' cleaning procedures may be more detailed, while others might be concerningly lax.

Still, it is reasonable for guests to expect a clean, functioning space. While a little smudge on a window might not be completely abhorrent to your guests, they will still expect clean floors, surfaces, dishes, and linens. While you may be able to live with a little mess in your own home, your guests definitely don't want to see someone else's dirty laundry and messes left behind, or deal with pet hair build-up, pests, or thick layers of grime.

One very generous exception would be for rustic stays, such as campsites, cabins, and motorhomes. In these instances, it's unrealistic to expect wildlife and insects to mind their own business. That's not to say a camper full of roaches gets a pass, but guests should expect to see an ant, spider, or small rodent within the proximity of the property, especially if they leave food out. The possibility of close encounters with nature – and helpful information about deterring pests – should still be noted on the property description, since some guests may be trying out this type of vacation for the first time. Again, it's important to set expectations and communicate as thoroughly as possible.

7: Parking and Transportation

What about parking? If you have a dedicated garage or parking space, this is no big deal, but what about those who rely on-street parking? Suppose you find yourself parking several blocks away from your home regularly. In that case, you might want to offer luggage drop-off services for your guests or suggest they take public transportation or rideshare to your location.

If you do have dedicated parking, you'll need to make sure the area is clean and in good repair. Any codes, passes, stickers, or transponders required for parking will also need to be shared with the guest immediately, so they can take full advantage of the opportunity to safely stow their car during their stay.

Transportation around your location is also a critical factor. Finding the way to the grocery store might be easy for you (or anyone with a passing knowledge of your area), but what about for people from out of state or even out of the country? Are streets well-marked? Can someone with a basic GPS or map feature on their cell phone get around? Is public transportation an option in your location? Your guests may not be familiar with how to find and use services like buses, taxis, trains, or subways. While it's not your responsibility to teach them how to use public transportation in your location, it is a good idea to share important transportation information, such as where to find details about routes, prices, and hours of operation.

On the other hand, if public transportation is not available in your location, this is another crucial detail to share with future guests. They may be used to hailing an Uber whenever they leave the house, so if Ubers do not service your area, they may have trouble getting around without advanced notice of this fact.

Think about the location of your rental space from the standpoint of someone who has never been to your area before. This can include details like navigating shared driveways and parking complexes, the distance to the closest bus stop or train terminal, or which cab service is most reliable. Including helpful details to your guests can make a huge difference in the success of your future Airbnb.

8: Can You Afford It?

Last, but certainly not least, you'll want to consider the financial implications of renting out your home. Obviously "profit = good," but there is an initial investment that comes with becoming an Airbnb host. You may want to purchase protective covers for some of your furniture or select linens and towels that will only be available for guests. You may choose to have professional cleaners come in between stays, or on a regular basis, to ensure everything is flawless. You'll be doing more laundry and buying more cleaning products. If you have a lawn, driveway, patio, or balcony, you'll want to make sure that they're safe and functional when you invite guests into your home.

You'll want to check with your insurance company to make sure you and your guests are covered. This goes doubly so if you have an outdoor feature like a pool, hot tub, or pond, that could be dangerous to an inexperienced party. Liability coverage is the specific part of a homeowner's policy that provides a payout for any damage or injury to your guests while they're on your property. No one enjoys having to think about all the bad things that could potentially happen in your home, but what if someone falls down your steps or slips in your shower? No matter how careful everyone is, accidents do happen, and it's important to know that you won't be putting your home or livelihood at risk.

Property insurance is another consideration for hosts. What if your guests accidentally cause a fire or flooding? Or, what if there's a fire, flood, or natural disaster in your home while the staying there? What if there is a theft or an act of vandalism while guests are staying in your home? Who is covered, and for how much?

Airbnb does provide Host Protection Insurance, which acts as primary liability insurance coverage. According to Airbnb's FAQ page, this provides coverage for injuries to guests, their property, and your neighborhood, as adjudged your responsibility by the local laws. However, there are exceptions. Some locations are not eligible for this coverage. In addition, those who host Airbnb "Experiences" and stays that are booked through certain sites are also exempt. We will be discussing more about how Airbnb protects hosts in greater detail in a later section.

While it is fantastic that Airbnb provides protection for hosts, it's important to review your local laws and insurance policy to make sure you have all the coverage you need to feel safe and secure in opening your home to guests.

The requirements, implications, and impact of insurance on your overall expenses is definitely something you'll want to investigate thoroughly. While the likelihood of something terrible happening isn't staggering, forgoing insurance coverage on your Airbnb could be infinitely more costly on you as the homeowner. For both hosts and their guests, it's better to be safe than sorry.

9: Airbnb Fees and Taxes

Whether your motivation for becoming an Airbnb host is to make a little extra money or to become a full-time host, you'll need to be prepared for the fees and tax implications of having a rental property.

The first thing you need to do is determine what you should expect when it comes to fees and taxes. Airbnb has not published an actual fee schedule, as there are some exceptions to the norm. Additionally, taxes can vary from one location to another, even if they're in the same region. Furthermore, it is entirely possible that things will have changed since publication of this book. Bear in mind that other hosting services will charge different fees, and may have a completely different fee schedule or process than Airbnb, so always check the fine print before starting the listing process.

Airbnb fees help cover the costs of running the site, including providing 24/7 support for hosts and guests, and assisting in marketing, to name just a few of the services covered by these fees. Hosts can choose to pay these fees in their entirety, or share them with guests in a split-fee model.

When hosts choose to pay the fee in its entirety, they can be looking at a number ranging between 14-16% of the subtotal for the total booking cost. This means the fee will be calculated before taxes are figured in, and deducted from the total amount the host would make on the booking. Let's say you choose to rent out your place for four nights, at a cost of $100 per night, and charge a one-time $50 cleaning fee. The total for the stay would be $450 before taxes. If the host pays Airbnb a 15% host fee, that means $67.50 of that would go to Airbnb to cover the service fee.There are some instances in which this is the only option hosts may have, based on the location of the property.

The split-fee model allows hosts to share the fees with their guests. Typically, the host will pay a 3% fee on the subtotal, while guests will be asked to pay a fee that can range all the way up to 14.2%. Hosts do not have input into what guests will be charged for their portion of the service fee, nor do they see the amount, though Airbnb does communicate the fee to guests at time of booking.

Additional fees can be incurred if hosts use the Super Strict cancellation policy, too. This is an invitation-only program that requires guests to notify of any cancellations 30 or 60 days prior to the check-in date in order to receive a 50% refund. There is an additional 2% service fee for hosts using this feature.

Then there are the tax implications of rental income. Policies and procedures vary around the world, of course, so be sure to sit down with your accountant or tax advisor for the specifics before you get started. The information provided in this book is in no way to be used as financial advice, since there are many factors in the equation which can change over time.

In the United States, the ins and outs of taxes and rental properties are a little complicated, but not entirely mysterious. The first number to remember is 14. If you rent out your primary home or vacation home for 14 days or fewer throughout the year, as long as you have personally spent 14 days or more in that particular location that year, you don't have to report your earnings to the IRS at all. Essentially, as long as you have considered that space your home for 14 days, you can rent it out for 14 days without any tax consequences. That being said, you cannot deduct your business expenses if you are utilizing this 14 day exception. You can deduct your mortgage interest and property tax, if you choose to itemize your taxes, but any expenses put into repairs, maintenance, furniture, and so forth cannot be deducted unless you rent your property more than 14 days in a year. In order to deduct it, you need to claim it, so to speak.

Airbnb will report your earnings to the IRS based on the number of bookings you have in a year and the total amount of income you made from those bookings. You'll receive a copy of IRS Form 1099-K, Payment Card and

Third Party Network Transactions. When you do your taxes, you'll definitely want to include the information on the 1099-K, since the IRS will be fully aware of the income you made through Airbnb.

In fact, Airbnb asks hosts to fill out an IRS W-9 Form right off the bat. This form asks hosts to share their own Taxpayer Identification Number (TIN) so that Airbnb is able to directly report income to the IRS. You can choose not to do this, but Airbnb will then withhold 28% of your income for each booking to cover tax responsibilities. Since your tax responsibility for each booking will generally be far less than 28%, it is highly beneficial to fill out and submit the W-9 quickly.

Airbnb income can either be reported on a Schedule C or Schedule E form, depending on your business model. If your goal is to become a full time rental entrepreneur, you'll look to Schedule C, which will require you to pay self-employment taxes. If instead you are casually renting a space and manage to book more than 14 nights in a year, you can complete Schedule E and avoid self-employment taxes.

This all may sound very complex, but there are plenty of resources that can help, including an accountant or tax professional. Just remember to keep incredibly detailed records and hold onto receipts. Business expenses associated with hosting an Airbnb space are tax deductible, including purchases made for food and other edible treats for your guests, maintenance and repair costs, cleaning costs, and the price of goods for all of the objects you buy for the rental space. As long as you stay organized and keep all of your expense records tidy, you should be able to recoup many of the expenses associated with getting your Airbnb up and running.

But what about occupancy taxes, value added taxes (VAT), and goods and services taxes (GST)? In some areas, hosts are required to collect an occupancy tax from guests. These vary on a regional and local level around the world. In many cases, Airbnb has been able to automate the collection of these taxes. When guests book a stay at your property they'll simply be charged automatically through the site, ensuring the host does not have to get involved.

There are a few areas in which taxes will need to be collected manually, by the hosts directly, outside of the Airbnb site. Hosts with access to the site's Professional Hosting tools can include the amount of tax due on their listings and collect this amount via the Resolution Center. Otherwise, hosts and guests will have to work out this process on their own. Airbnb doesn't have tools available to assist with manual collection of occupancy taxes, though it is recommended that this process be addressed prior to arrival, with taxes paid upon check-in.

As a prospective Airbnb host, you'll want to do some thorough research to ensure you're aware of your exact tax responsibilities. There are instances in which Airbnb is able to automate the regional taxes, but a local tax must be collected manually. Find out what your jurisdiction requires before you get started to avoid any unpleasant surprises come tax season.

As you were reading through the nine areas of consideration, hopefully you were able to note some very important decisions you must make. Perhaps this list jogged a few extra ideas or considerations specific to your lifestyle or location. The goal of this chapter was to help you gather all of the information you need to properly evaluate your home and situation before you start building your Airbnb experience for future guests. While more important decisions have been made with less forethought, being prepared can lead to greater success for you and, more importantly, greater comfort for your future guests.

Chapter 3: Your End Goal

As you consider the realities and possibilities of setting up your own Airbnb property, take a step back for a moment to think about *why* you're doing this. What is your end goal for being an Airbnb host?

For most people, the first response to this question is "to help people out and/or make a little money." On the surface, renting out an existing space is a great way to add a little income to your household. Renting out extra rooms or properties can help a space pay for itself over time. For example, that camper trailer you bought on a whim can be converted into a wise business investment, or renting out the second bedroom can help cover rent while you search for a longer term roommate.

As you can tell by now, becoming an Airbnb host is not a simple, cut-and-dry process where you can just toss your spare key under the mat and hope everything goes well. Instead, you need to make sure you have a clean, habitable, hospitable environment, and that you're prepared to troubleshoot problems that haven't even happened yet. Once you become a host, you need to be on your communication A Game at all times. Hosting is going to require a significant investment of time and money for you, at least at first.

Consider these two scenarios:

Scenario 1: You're renting out a spare room in your home. In theory, you could rent that room out every single day, 365 days a year, but that's not a reasonable expectation. Remember, people have to view your listing and book their stay with you, which will depend on location, popularity, local events, weather, and more factors entirely out of your control.

So let's say all of the stars align and you are able to book 20 nights each month. Take a look at what type of commitment you can expect out of each listing:

	Time	Money
Communication	– Average of 2 hours total per guest – Average of 1 hour per inquiry that does not result in a booking	– Nominal, unless internet/cell phone/data costs are expensive in your area
Cleaning	– Recommended average of one hour per room – Must be cleaned after and before each new stay	– -If a cleaning company is hired, approximately $100 per 1000 square foot,* potentially more for messier spaces – -If cleaning yourself, the cost of cleaning products/shampoos, gloves, sponges, rags, etc.
Check-In/Check-Out	– Time required to meet, provide or retrieve a key/parking information, to provide instructions, and to discuss any feedback – Approximately two hours total	– Cost of duplicate key or parking passes
Updating Listing	– Keep availability dates current, update check-in/check-out times based on your schedule, administrative work with Airbnb – -Estimated 10-20 hours each month	– Nominal, unless internet/cell phone/data costs are expensive in your area – However, there are con-siderable costs to both time and potential in-come for failure to keep your calendar current

*This will vary based on location and type of space

As you can see, the main monetary sacrifice occurs in the cleaning category. At minimum, you'll be investing in a spare key and an impressive array of cleaning products. The costs for a cleaning company can really add up over time but might be a nice added bonus if you regularly use the space as your own.

Time is the most significant sacrifice in becoming an Airbnb host, especially the time spent communicating with current and potential guests. There are some processes that can be automated for a fee through the website, but you'll still need to respond to any inquiries about your property in a prompt manner. Not all of these discussions will end in a booking either. From a business standpoint, you will likely spend more time answering questions from people who do not book a stay at your property than you will from those who proceed with the booking. Insufficient communication can result in poor ratings on your listing, which can lessen the probability of future bookings.

Overall, it's very difficult to classify Airbnb hosting as "passive" income since a lot of activity is required on your part.

Let's look at another scenario.

Scenario 2: You are renting out a dedicated property, such as a carriage house, cabin, campsite, RV, whole house, etc. You do not live on-site or do not plan to be onsite around the clock.

	Time	Money
Communication	- Average of 2 hours total per guest - Average of 1 hour per inquiry that does not result in a booking	- Nominal, unless internet/cell phone/data costs are expensive in your area
Cleaning/Upkeep	- Recommended average of one hour per room - Must be cleaned after and before each new stay - Transit time - Regular repairs/maintenance - Time necessary to personally stop by, lay eyes on the site, and make sure all is in good order	- -If a cleaning company is hired, approximately $100 per 1000 square foot,* potentially more for messier spaces - -If cleaning yourself, the cost of cleaning products/shampoos, gloves, sponges, rags, etc. - -Cost of commute to/from site - Cost of repairs/maintenance - -Cost of furniture/supplies as appropriate
Check-In/Check-Out	- Time required to meet, provide or retrieve a key/parking information, to provide instructions, and to discuss any feedback - Approximately two hours total	- Cost of duplicate key or parking passes - Commute to/from the site - Cost of security equipment to allow/automate access (optional)
Updating Listing	- Keep availability dates current, update check-in/check-out times based on your schedule, administrative work with Airbnb - Estimated 10-20 hours each month	- Nominal, unless internet/cell phone/data costs are expensive in your area - However, there are considerable costs to both time and potential income for failure to keep your calendar current - Cancellations if problems are detected

*This will vary based on location and type of space

All of the commitments from the first scenario have carried over, but now there are a few fun new additions.

Renting a property you own but do not reside in brings with it a separate list of challenges, but also unique benefits. While you may be thrilled that you won't have to share a space with a stranger, you do have to accept that you will need to visit the location frequently to make sure it's clean and appropriate for Airbnb guests. You don't want to assume that all of the standard features of your camper are in order, only to find out when your guests arrive that the entire vehicle is buried under the trunk of a fallen tree, for example.

You can automate the check-in/check-out process by providing lockboxes, keypad-operated locks, security system codes, or other remote processes, which can save you time driving back and forth to and from your property. These remote measures will include a higher associated cost than duplicating your key. While the extra security may bring with it a little peace of mind, there will be bills related to installation, operation, and any monitoring of security devices.

There's also the matter of upkeep. When you actually live in your Airbnb rental, you know what's going on at all times. The furniture in the space is yours, and you use it every day. You know where everything belongs, and how it should look. From the forks and knives to the linens and ice trays, everything in your space is likely used every day. Furthermore, if a window seal begins to leak or the air conditioner goes out, you're aware of it immediately.

When it comes to the upkeep of a property that is not your main residence, you need to be on the ball at all times. That means frequent check-ins to make sure everything is in good repair and working order. That also means furnishing the place and providing reasonable amenities. In some cases, such as a rustic campsite rental, that may not go much further than paying the season's fees. But unless your listing is a unique experience that specifies otherwise, you'll need to provide some type of sleeping arrangement, toilet, and a way to source or make food.

In most cases, these will be one-time or very infrequent purchases, such as furniture and linens. However, things like toilet paper, the cost of laundering the linens, and utilities will add up significantly over time. For example, suppose you decide to provide your guests with the opportunity to make morning coffee. In that case, the one-time investment of a coffee pot will soon be overshadowed by the cost of purchasing coffee, cream, sweeteners, or any other additions you want to offer. There will be a little math work involved with calculating how much of any given product you'll need based on volume of guests and standard usage. Buying some items in bulk may be a great way to save on costs, but this may not always be possible.

Now that you're more aware of the investment involved, let's revisit your end goal. Ask yourself these questions:

- Are you content to occasionally rent out or share your property with someone who is in town for a specific event?
- Do you *need* to make a specific amount of money each month to cover your expenses?
- Are you looking for a way to supplement your income, but it's not your top priority?
- Are you what's considered a budding rental entrepreneur, or "Rentrepreneur?" Meaning you're looking to make this a serious source of income in the future and either already have or plan to grow an entire portfolio of properties and concepts to attract a large range of potential renters.

All of these are valid reasons to delve into the world of Airbnb hosting; however, understanding your motivation will help you better plan out the next steps of your journey. As with any new source of income, you want to develop a business plan for how you envision renting will work. Communication is certainly key, as we've mentioned repeatedly, but organization is going to be incredibly important on your end as well. When hosting an Airbnb, you need to be at the right place at the right time in order to answer emails and in-person questions as quickly as possible. Many hosts compare it to being on a constant live feed with their guests. You'll have to coordinate every aspect of the stay to ensure your guests are comfortable and satisfied. Do you want to take that on as a full-time responsibility?

This section has given you a lot to think about when it comes to making your own space an Airbnb listing, but this is hardly a comprehensive list. You may think of many personal situations or scenarios that will be impacted by inviting others into your home temporarily. It is highly recommended that you jot down questions, thoughts, and ideas you have as they appear, especially in the early stages.

While it can be tempting to use Airbnb's simple process of creating a listing right away, you must step back for a moment to consider whether becoming a host is a good idea for your space, your lifestyle, and your overall goals. If you find any of these considerations lead you to a problem that's hard to solve, you may want to re-think whether this is the right time or place for you to begin your Airbnb career.

If you're still as excited as ever, the time has come to start conceptualizing your space.

SECTION 2: THE EXPERIENCE

When we say "The Experience," we don't necessarily mean what Airbnb categorizes as "Experiences." That is, we're specifically discussing the overall ambiance, functionality, and comfort guests experience from the moment they book your property to the publication of their public review, rather than "One-of-a-kind activities hosted by experts," as defined by Airbnb.

Traveling can be stressful, and depending on why your guests booked your property, they may be in no mood for any unpredictable hassles or shenanigans. That's why you have to think of what type of experience you want to provide to your guests ahead of time and make sure you budget your own time and money to ensure it goes according to plan. This goes beyond the basic furniture you use. It's also a matter of what amenities are provided, along with any conveniences and extras that might enhance your guests' overall experience. Before you even create the listing, you have to think about what you want to do with your space. What do you want to provide to your guests? What fits within the space itself? What's your intended usage?

Each type of property may offer a different type of experience. A cabin in the woods might be very rustic and bare-bones, with a fire pit and nearby outhouse, but you still want guests to know what to expect and appreciate every aspect of their stay. You'll want to be careful not to under or over sell your property when you finally create your listing, so think carefully about how much you want to offer. Most guests will be forgiving if, for instance, your WiFi goes down in a storm, but if you specifically mention the amazing hot tub at your place and it is unusable when guests arrive, you can bet someone will complain.

The good news is that setting expectations is entirely within your control. Once posted, your listing can be edited, so if the hot tub goes on the fritz, or you're no longer able to source your signature single-origin coffee, you can make sure your online listing accurately reflects what you do and don't offer. These extra amenities and your attention to detail in communicating what your guests can look forward to will be a major factor in how your guests evaluate their stay. This is your chance to really shine and watch those bookings multiply... if you so choose.

Chapter 1: Creating the Setting

By "setting," we don't just mean the color scheme and furniture style. This term extends to the entirety of the property, both in form and function. Not only do you need to decide what type of space you'll provide, you'll need to establish the boundaries of how and when it can be used. This is equally important whether it's a space you'll share or a dedicated rental property. You want to ensure everyone has a good time, but also a safe time.

Please note that if you plan to rent a simple space, such as a campsite or rustic cabin, much of this won't apply to your particular situation. However, on the off chance that you decide to expand in the future, or if you decide to elevate your space, you may want to glance at some of the basics to designing a cozy and hospitable Airbnb.

Step 1: Evaluating the Space

First, take a look at the space you want to list on Airbnb. Take measurements. Pay attention to where the windows and doors are and any natural light. Knowing which areas receive natural light is more important than you might think, especially in bedrooms. Most people don't want the sun to rise in their faces, nor do they want to have doors potentially opening into their face or knees if the space has an awkward flow.

If this is a space you have lived in, or will share, you might not be willing or capable of changing the traffic flow or furniture placement. However, see what you can do to maximize space without minimizing movement. Remember, these individuals have never been to this space. They'll need a moment to familiarize themselves with the layout. They may be carrying bulky luggage when they first walk through. If you decide to allow pets, you might want to keep some things out of muzzle, paw, and tail reach.

This may be time to assess the accessibility of your space in more detail. Do you have hallways that can be navigated by wheelchairs, walkers, or other mobility devices? Look for areas where you might have had to squeeze through or step over something to avoid colliding with furniture or walls with strange angles. For example, perhaps your dining room chairs are squeezed very tightly between the wall and table. Or maybe the closet door and bedroom door cannot be opened simultaneously due to the room's layout.

This is not to say that having tight or irregular angles in your home should prevent you from placing your listing on Airbnb. It just means you want to be sure to minimize and mitigate any potential accidents and inconveniences. While you can't change the angle between the closet and bedroom doors, you can re-evaluate the furniture in your dining room space. As you look around your home, ask yourself if there is a temporary option that might be more user-friendly.

Making your home "user-friendly" might entail getting rid of extra fixtures that obstruct the room's flow or moving furniture to accommodate more movement. Consider this: you have a fold-out sofa, but it's currently trapped behind a coffee table. Would it be worth figuring out new placement for that sofa or coffee table, if it meant increasing the number of guests you could host at a time, potentially growing your popularity as a host?

As you can see in this evaluation process, the earlier step of determining your end goal in renting your space on Airbnb is a very valuable part of the decisions you make. If you aren't interested in becoming a rental entrepreneur, then perhaps it is not worth it to move your furniture around. On the other hand, if you're looking to make this a reliable source of income, you might look at a room from the perspective of hosting more guests simultaneously, along with a way to streamline the space so that it's easier and faster to clean in between rapid-fire reservations.

Step 2: Furnishing for Function

Once you've considered each room of the space you're renting or potentially sharing, it's time to examine the furniture. If you're starting with an empty room or house, this can be both intimidating and exciting, as you have the ability to start from scratch. If you already have basic furnishing in the space, your job is to make sure everything in the room is clean, functional, and useful.

Adding to a room is much easier than subtracting, but the principle is the same: make sure that the contents of the room are appropriate for its purpose. That doesn't mean each room should be devoid of decor and personality, but these aspects of the overall experience aren't at the top of the priority list. First, you want to make sure that everything is clean. Inexplicable stains, smells, and strange sticky spots are not going to earn you high reviews. Your guests should not be inspired to hose down everything with antibacterial spray.

Likewise, broken fixtures don't leave a great impression. You want to be certain all of the furniture pieces can do their job without danger of collapse or dysfunction. Drawers need to open, doors need to shut, and sitting in chairs and lying down in beds shouldn't feel like a funhouse ride. Make sure everything is stable and sturdy.

As mentioned in the previous step, your guests need the flow of your space to make sense. You want to ensure they don't damage your property or themselves, or get lost trying to find the bathroom in the middle of the night. Look at the furniture in each room to determine if it serves a purpose, or if it just takes up space.

Remember also that your guests will have luggage with them. Where can they put it, so they aren't constantly tripping over it? Can you offer them some drawers or designated closet space? What if they need to hang something up? While this may seem like a lot to consider for the average overnight guest, you have to be able to anticipate these types of questions and be able to provide a response, even if that response is, "I'm sorry, I don't have that available."

Step 3: Adding Decor

Aesthetic additions should follow the same guidelines from step two. Adding a decorative vase, knick-knack, or wall art is a fantastic idea, but make sure that the guest doesn't spend more time trying to keep the vase safe than they do enjoying their stay.

Make sure the decor is appropriate to the type of environment you're trying to cultivate too. If you have a downtown party loft in the bar district, perhaps a priceless Venetian sculpture is not the right vibe. If you are touting your space as "kid-friendly," minimize the number of breakables within reach of tiny hands.

Many Airbnb hosts use decor and aesthetics as a selling point for their listings. But again, your willingness and ability to go to extremes on this end depends on your end game. If you're renting the spare bedroom in your apartment on an as-needed basis, you might furnish the room with a bed, a dresser, and a chair, with tasteful wall art and be perfectly satisfied with the results. On the other hand, if you plan to go for full rental entrepreneur status, you might want to start considering room themes, color schemes, and inspiration boards. The most important thing to keep in mind is your ability and willingness to make this a considerable investment rather than a fun side project.

Step 4: Establishing Important Boundaries

Lastly, create boundaries with your space. This is equally important for those who will be actively sharing their home with guests as those who will not be present for the duration of the stay. Establishing boundaries regarding how your space can and should be used is very important to ensuring everyone has an enjoyable experience. This way, you won't have to worry about guests doing something inappropriate or inconvenient. Don't expect your guests to ask permission; instead, share your expectations right away.

For example, it is not unreasonable to ask guests not to smoke indoors or have overnight guests. It is also quite common and understandable to ask that women's hygiene products not be flushed in the toilet, as that could cause the toilet to back up or damage the plumbing. If you don't want guests to put their feet on the sofa, open windows, or crank the heater up to inferno levels, you can specify these requests and limitations. We'll discuss creating and communicating hard and fast rules later in this book, but these are some common requirements that you might wish to put on your listing, especially if there are dire consequences, such as pipes bursting or fuses blowing.

Additionally, if you're sharing a space, you will want to set boundaries about shared areas, such as bathrooms, kitchens, and living quarters. This goes both ways, of course. Your guest expects to be able to use the toilet whenever they need to, just as you expect to be able to have full access to the bathroom to get ready for work in the morning. Communicating these needs is always the easiest way to eliminate avoidable stress.

Creating "the setting" may seem as simple as picking out some tasteful furniture, coming up with a few items that match, and fluffing the pillows before guests arrive, but it encompasses so much more. You want to ensure that the space you invite guests into is clean, hospitable and navigable, not cluttered or overwhelming to guests. Remember that for your guests, this is all very new and exciting, so try to consider their point of view when creating the experience.

Chapter 2: Amenities

The next thing to consider is what amenities you can – and will – offer. Amenities are those little things that go over and above the expectations of a bed, bathroom, and place to prepare food, and they can contribute quite a bit to the frequency of the bookings you receive through Airbnb.

Unless they are specifically looking for a rustic or wilderness-like experience, guests absolutely love amenities. The more "bonus" features they're offered, the higher the likelihood of people choosing your space over similar spots in your area.

The good news is that not only does providing a greater number of amenities make you more competitive in the Airbnb market, but it also gives you a reasonable opportunity to raise your rates. We'll discuss how to set your rates and pricing later in this book, but bear in mind that if cost is a factor in your willingness to share certain amenities, you will very likely recoup your expenses.

Some of the most popular amenities are those that help travelers replicate the feeling of being home, such as cable TV or streaming services, WiFi, and access to a laundry room. Even the most seasoned traveler can appreciate kicking off their shoes at the end of the night and relaxing in front of a familiar movie before going to bed.

What you can offer may depend quite a bit on the type of space and experience you intend to provide. For example, if your Airbnb property is a family-friendly cabin far from the cell phone signals of the city, you might want to throw in a television and DVD player so the family can gather around and watch movies together. If you're renting a tiny house, you may not be able to offer a full-sized refrigerator or indoor bathroom, but you can provide a small cooler or a camp toilet and outdoor bathing area.

Below is a list of some common amenities to help generate ideas when it comes to evaluating and preparing your own Airbnb property. This list is certainly not exhaustive, and some options may not relate or make sense to your space. Instead, this list is designed to get your thoughts jump-started and organized so you can make your listing the best it can possibly be.

Amenity	Available	Unavailable
Freezer		
Ice Maker		
Washer/Dryer		
Bathtub		
WiFi		
Television		
Dishwasher		

Additionally, this is another situation in which you should decide what makes sense in the context of a short-term stranger staying in your space. If, for example, the washing machine is prone to going off-balance unless you offer it a specific supplication, you may want to simplify matters by saying the laundry is off-limits or out of order. Likewise, if the television remote control process involves more than six steps, you may want to consider how you'll address that with your guests.

As with everything involved in hosting, communication will save you plenty of time and energy. You'll have the ability to explain what is and is not included in your listing. While you don't need to explain *why* the television is off-limits or justify your decision, it is a good idea to be upfront in the listing about the lack of a certain amenity, especially if it is an extremely popular feature that some might naturally expect or take for granted.

Chapter 3: What is included?

For each amenity you offer, make sure you ask yourself, *"What's included? What do I need to enjoy this fully?"*

On the surface, the question seems a little silly. What do you need to "enjoy" a television, except the remote, electricity, and a channel decent enough to keep your attention for approximately twenty minutes? In fact, the television may be one of the more straightforward amenities to customize for that very reason. You can make sure the remote has batteries, sanitize the remote after each guest, and you're pretty much set. Or you can go the extra mile by enabling casting from devices, creating a Netflix account just for your guests, and making sure the television itself doesn't have a glare from one of the windows, so your guests can watch their programs at any time of day they like. You get to decide whether you provide the bare minimum or the full experience when it comes to your amenities.

Generally speaking, it's a good idea to anticipate some of the needs of your guests. Most people don't travel with a full set of sheets and towels, so providing linens for the bed, along with bath towels, hand towels, and washcloths, is an excellent idea. Obviously, if this is a campsite or otherwise lacks a traditional bed or bathroom, these will not be necessary.

Similarly, dish towels and dishwashing tools, like sponges and detergents, are a fantastic addition for kitchen spaces, when applicable. Some hosts provide a fully-stocked, fully-functional kitchen, as well. Pots, pans, plates, utensils, and even cooking and serving tools like spatulas and ladles can be extremely helpful to guests who are passing through but still crave a homemade meal.

If a coffee maker is one of your offered amenities, you'll want to provide filters, coffee grounds or pods, and mugs. Some hosts expand this by providing tea bags, creamer, sugar and/or alternative sweeteners, and more. You can offer a setup that consists of a tin of instant coffee, a mug, and a tea kettle to boil water, or you can create an elaborate at-home coffee bar with various flavor selections and additional options for upgrading the coffee experience, such as flavor pumps, a creamer array, and so on.

Paper goods are also a good idea, especially if you want to encourage guests to maintain a clean home. Toilet paper is non-negotiable, but bonus items like paper towels, disinfectant wipes, and tissues can be very helpful as well. Even the most cautious guest can accidentally tip over a beverage or get a runny nose, and providing them with an easy, disposable method of remedying the situation right away will prevent a tiny mess from becoming a big problem in the long run. You don't necessarily need to provide the guest with a complete cleaning kit, but some basic mess mitigation can be helpful for everyone.

The list of possibilities goes on and on as you attempt to make your space as hospitable as possible: hand soap at the sinks, a complimentary bar of soap in the shower, shampoo, a hair dryer, an iron, detergent for the laundry, an umbrella in case it rains, and games or books for the whole family.

Before you go completely overboard, think about the space and what's appropriate. If you're actively living in the space, your included offerings might be a little more robust, as they're part of your daily functioning household. That doesn't mean, however, you are required to share absolutely everything you own.

Think of the various hotels, motels, and inns you may have visited during your own travels. Each one provided different amenities and extras, depending on the overall vibe and intended experience. Most likely, the cost of the hotel room and the number of cool freebies you expected were directly related. The higher the cost, the more extras. Apply this concept to your Airbnb space, as well. While you can certainly choose to provide a few cotton swabs if the guest inquires about them, you don't have to offer a full range of cosmetic sponges and wipes.

Remember too that all of these amenities cost money. Your desire to be kind and accommodating will add up quickly. Plus, you'll have to continually ensure you've got plenty of each included item in stock. Your guests may quickly use up all of a certain product. You are making this feature available for the guests to use as they see fit, which might mean the coffee remains untouched, or the laundry detergent might be completely depleted by the end of the week. That can translate into last-minute runs to the store and continuous and potentially unpredictable expenses.

Keep your budget in mind at all times, and pay attention to any trends in how guests use the items you share with them. You can always make changes and adjustments. For example, if you notice your kitchen is constantly left in disarray, perhaps you add a dish rack with a dedicated scrubber wand and detergent to encourage dishwashing.

Creating a hospitable, functional environment for your guests can lead you down a rabbit hole of "what if" scenarios, but your goal is not to anticipate every potential need your guests may have but rather to make sure the space is functional and enjoyable with what is on hand.

Chapter 4: Extras

Beyond all of the everyday, functional things you'll offer guests, there's also the concept of "extras" to be addressed.

Some hosts choose to provide their guests with a little extra touch. Doing so endears them to the guests, and adds a competitive edge among the myriad of Airbnb properties in the area. And besides, if you've had a long day of wearying travel, wouldn't you love a little human acknowledgment?

The concept is nothing new or exclusive to Airbnbs. Hotels have been leaving mints on pillows seemingly since the dawn of recorded history. These tiny tokens of appreciation are often just the right touch to help bring a smile to the faces of exhausted travelers who may be nervous about starting their exploration of your location.

Food is a popular extra, especially items like bottled water or a small, non-perishable snack. If you live in an area known for a special treat, you might leave a sample in the bedroom or refrigerator. A bottle of wine or local beer is also a common choice. Some hosts even provide fresh-cut flowers throughout the house. A well-placed power strip can mean the world to someone working on the road. Something as simple as a personalized note thanking them for their visit and business can be endearing and meaningful to tired travelers.

If you're welcoming pets, you might want to include the pets in the extras, with a yummy treat or a water bowl ready to go. You can provide doggie clean-up bags, or a litter box for cats, too.

As a host, you don't want to provide something that will spoil or create a mess, but rather something that will acknowledge and welcome your guest. However, you don't want to make a substantial financial investment in the extras, either. Some of the most popular extras are inexpensive yet helpful and meaningful for guests. Creative extras are particularly fun if you have a property that's extraordinary, or in an interesting location. For example, you can create a guest book to allow each guest to share their experience in your space. You choose to offer tours to your guests, or find other inventive ways to show off your living space or the surrounding area. If your Airbnb is on a working farm, invite guests to meet the animals or offer them a sample of your seasonal harvest.

Guide books are also a thoughtful addition to your Airbnb. Bearing in mind that many guests have never visited your town before, you can choose to create a book of local destinations to help them get around. Sure, they could Google all of that before they arrive, but many people would love to hear what restaurants are recommended by the locals or what shops and activities are considered a "must-see." This can also include practical information such as the local gas station with the widest array of snacks or the pharmacy that's generally expedient when filling prescriptions. You can include a list of restaurants that deliver to your property, great places to walk a dog, or all of the above!

In addition to guide books, you might want to provide details about public transportation in your area. As discussed earlier, your guests with less public transportation experience could make obvious mistakes ranging from making incorrect assumptions about availability to having absolutely no clue how it works. A map of local bus stops or train stops can be helpful, along with the phone numbers for any cab companies. Some hosts will leave a partially loaded transport card to help get guests started exploring the area. At the very least you want to make sure the address of your Airbnb is plainly posted within the house. If your guests hire a rideshare or order delivery food, they'll want to be absolutely certain of the address.

You may also consider writing up a brief history of your property. Writing this out is especially compelling for guests if you live in a unique structure or historic part of town. There's a bit of a history buff in many of us, so getting perspective on the history of your home can be extremely interesting to travelers. It can also help them feel more in touch and connected with their surroundings, which can significantly benefit them when treading unfamiliar waters.

One recommendation shared by long-time Airbnb hosts is to be consistent. Guests like things to be cohesive and make sense. For example, if you're going for the eco/green vibe, don't offer your guests plastic utensils and disposable plates. If you're creating a luxurious getaway, don't provide ratty towels that have seen better days. Details are the key to satisfying your guests, so if you can't keep everything at the same standard of quality, cleanliness, and functionality, it might be best to skip it altogether.

Remember to not overwhelm your guests with "too much." This may seem confusingly counter-intuitive after reading about "extras." Still, there's a big difference between a stack of clutter that takes up every possible surface, and a tasty chocolate treat waiting on the nightstand.

While reading this section you may have begun to feel exasperated or overwhelmed, but remember that these extras are elective. You don't *have* to do any of these things or do them for every guest. Items like guidebooks and transportation maps are relatively permanent since you only need to make updates in the event of change. The history of your property won't change, so that's a minor investment of time as well. Otherwise, you can choose to spend a little extra or not. Perhaps you save these extra touches for guests who have divulged that their stay is to celebrate a special occasion. You can start small and build your overall aesthetic and ambiance over time, as your resources permit.

The wonderful thing about creating the experience is it's entirely within your control. Yes, you want to provide your guests with the basic necessities, but you don't have to splurge for luxury touches unless you are specifically looking to deliver a five-star experience.

Creating your Airbnb experience can be incredibly fun, especially if you have a local theme in mind for your space. However, you don't need to go overboard to please your guests. Stick with keeping everything clean, functional, and necessary, and then build your experience from there. Impress guests with your warm welcome rather than the thread count of your sheets. Feel free to make your Airbnb unique, but don't lose sight of the real purpose here: to create a hospitable place for travelers to sleep, bathe, and eat.

CATION
CHECK IN
Add dates
New York
City in New York, United States
New York County
County in New York, United States
New Jersey

SECTION 3: HOUSE MANUAL, CHECK-IN, AND RULES

As we've stressed several times so far, communication between host and guest is crucial. Each host is responsible for creating an Airbnb posting that accurately represents the space. Likewise, every guest should feel empowered to ask any questions they might have about a property they may potentially rent.

Everyone has different needs and preferences. While it would be impossible for each host to address and fulfill every potential request, it is vital to communicate what can and cannot be done.

As a host, you will most likely not be around every moment to provide your guests with guidance and information. True, the Airbnb app makes it incredibly easy and efficient for hosts and guests to communicate back and forth before, during, and after their stay. Still, it would be an impressive feat to fully express all of your requests and requirements via text. Sometimes we don't think of things until the very last minute.

You can take certain measures to help your guests out and provide yourself with a little extra peace of mind. House manuals are one way that you can continuously communicate with your guests, even if you're nowhere near the site. The check-in process can also be a great time to discuss any of the concerns held by either party. Lastly, clearly posting house rules can give you some additional leverage in enforcing any requirements you may have as the host and owner of the property.

Chapter 1: House Manual

A house manual is something that Airbnb strongly encourages for all hosts. The manual doesn't have to be a lengthy tome but should still clear up all of the things guests need to know to enhance their comfort, and keep you from worrying too much or fielding a flood of late night messages.

Start the manual out with the basics. The manual should include the address of the property, your contact information, and any important details such as the names of other individuals in the home or on the property, details regarding any resident pets, and any particular notes that might be helpful about comings and goings on the property. For example, if the lawn service appears every Wednesday at 8 am, that might be a good heads up for guests who like to sleep in late. If a roommate works third shift, this might be another critical thing to point out, so guests aren't concerned about an intruder. Emergency contact information should be present here as well, which we'll discuss in detail in a later chapter.

Next, include pertinent information for first-time visitors to your home, such as where to find towels and linens, bathroom supplies, and kitchenware. You can also include instructions on how to use the television and other appliances, such as the washer and dryer. If there are any particular recommendations about these amenities, such as "the washer does best on cold" or "when the TV first comes on, the volume will be low; adjust as needed," the house manual is an excellent place to inform your guests.

Additionally, this is a fantastic way to share details like WiFi passwords, gate codes, and other personal and secure details that might enhance their overall stay. Thermostat instructions or unlock codes for secure devices are another good thing to share. Suppose you have a home assistant device, such as an Amazon Alexa or Google Home. In that case, you should disclose this in the house manual to prevent any confusion, especially if the guest has a mobile version of the app installed on their personal devices. It might become super frustrating for a guest to shout "Hey Google," and have multiple assistants respond simultaneously.

Lastly, if specific things are off-limits or out of bounds, make sure this is mentioned in the house manual. You'll also want to post these in the house rules, as we'll discuss shortly, but some things cannot be reiterated enough. For example, failure to clearly and frequently remind guests that there is no garbage disposal could result in undue damage from a guest attempting to shove scraps through your plumbing. Likewise, if there are shared areas in your home, the house manual is the place to share any rules or respectful tidbits for sharing these spaces. This includes what items in the refrigerator are up for grabs, when the bathroom will not be available to guests, or when the television is off-limits.

At first you may feel that the house manual is a bit overboard, but as you begin hosting you'll feel much more at ease knowing that you have provided your guests with a step-by-step, up-to-date guide on how they can achieve maximum comfort in your space. While it will not eliminate a potential barrage of questions from your guests, you will be able to assuage much of the anxiety they may experience in an unfamiliar home in a new location.

Chapter 2: Check-In and Check-Out

Hosts can also take advantage of the check-in process as a way to give your guests a brief orientation of your premises. Some hosts have automated the check-in process, with door or security codes texted to guests prior to arrival. But for those who will need to meet guests in person to provide a key or parking pass, the check-in process can be an excellent time for a meet and greet, along with a brief walkthrough to answer any immediate questions.

Before your guests arrive, you'll want to establish a check-in time. Most hosts determine this time based on cleaning requirements, especially if they have back-to-back stays booked. Hosts can indicate check-in times on their listing and in early communications to guests. The most popular way to communicate the check-in time is to provide the time and a short rationale, such as, "Check-in time is set at 5:00 pm local time to allow for thorough cleaning."

But what should you do if your guests arrive before your set check-in time? Some hosts consider this a problem outside of their realm of responsibility. Others allow for luggage drop off and storage and may even provide recommendations of fun activities to do nearby while they await the appropriate check-in time.

Luggage drop-off may also be helpful if parking is not guaranteed or is potentially distant from your home. Many guests may feel uncomfortable hauling their giant suitcases through block after block of unfamiliar city streets, so coordinating a drop-off ahead of time can definitely ease this process for them. Again, this is not a requirement but a kind gesture that can win over weary travelers and gain glowing reviews for your property.

When putting together your check-in process, here are the main tips for communicating with your visitors before their visit:

- What time will they check-in?
- Who will be present (if anyone)?
- How will they get their key?
- Where should they leave a car?
- How is luggage getting from their car to the house (do you allow luggage drop-off)?

Check-out should be a similar process. You'll want to set a check-out time that allows you adequate time to clean and check your space before the next guest arrives, but without rushing people too much. Many Airbnb hosts take a cue from hotels and establish a check-out time between 10 am and noon, allowing guests to get plenty of rest, clean up, and pack before leaving.

Many of the same process-related questions from check-in apply to check-out as well. In addition, you may wish to be present at check-out to address any concerns personally, receive feedback about the stay, and to collect any keys or parking devices. You'll also want to coordinate with guests if they'll need to fetch their car from a remote parking area to pick up their luggage.

The check-in and check-out process can certainly be automated, which might be very helpful for you as the host, especially if you have places you need to be or live off-site. However, this can also be a key opportunity to introduce yourself personally, provide guidance regarding your property, and share any tips or rules you have established for your home.

Chapter 3: Rules

As a new Airbnb host, you may feel like establishing rules for your guests is a bit nit-picky and invasive. However, as a property owner, you'll need to set rules and boundaries for everyone's safety and enjoyment.

While we like to think of our guests as kind, well-behaved, respectful people, things can happen. People come from different backgrounds, and what is perfectly acceptable in their normal situation may be strictly off-limits in your home. Additionally, some people enter a "vacation state of mind" when traveling and do things they normally wouldn't do in everyday life, such as drink too much, stay out too late, or party like rock stars. While you certainly want your guests to feel comfortable enjoying themselves and having a good time, you do need to lay down the law, so to speak, to provide safety and security for everyone involved.

Your rules will vary based on your space and your personal preferences, but here are a few topics to get you started on establishing your guidelines:

- Pets

- Smoking
- Drinking alcohol
- Guests other than the persons on the reservation
- Other household residents
- Use of amenities
- Neighborhood regulations (quiet hours, parking require-ments)
- Fire pit/cooking out restrictions

Most hosts post this on their booking confirmation in addition to including it in the house manual.

There are a few additional ways to encourage good behavior from your guests, as well. If you want them to take off their shoes at the door, try leaving a shoe rack or tray by the door, or a chair to help those who might need a hand removing and putting shoes back on. If keeping dishes clean is a huge priority, be sure to leave out dish detergent and scrubbing tools or have a dishwasher available for guests to load prior to departure. If you don't want to deal with makeup stains on your towels and linens, offer makeup removal cloths for your guests. Are you worried about rings on the furniture? Leave out coasters, or ask guests to keep food and beverages in designated eating areas. Make it as easy as possible for them to follow the rules, so you'll be met with less resistance and fewer excuses.

This might go without saying, but don't put out any objects you don't want touched. If something is very dear to you and you would be devastated if it broke or disappeared, lock it up. This is not to say all guests are liars, thieves, and mischief-makers, but accidents happen. Any item on display is subject to being touched, picked up, or moved by a guest. If pets are invited into your Airbnb space, take into account any tails, teeth, or ram-bunctious behavior that might impact your decor and furniture.

Labeling your cabinets and drawers is also a helpful way to guide visitors around your property. It may seem like overkill, but think of the time and energy saved by finding a drinking glass behind a door labeled "Drinking Glasses" rather than shuffling through every cabinet in the house.

Lastly, don't expect guests to read your mind. If you have specific preferences, share them. Providing a house manual and rules will save everyone time and frustration in the long run. Guests will know what to expect and have access to answers to their questions, while you'll rest easy knowing that you have shared all of the important

information for optimal enjoyment of your space.

SECTION 4: WHEN THINGS GO WRONG

Now that we've discussed the process of Airbnb hosting from the perspective of your own preparations and perspectives, it's time to consider that not every booking will be sunshine and daisies.

What should you do when things go awry? How do you plan for accidentals, incidentals, and criminal activity? What are some warning signs you should look for? And even more importantly, what type of protection is available for you and your guests when things go sideways?

First, it's important to recognize the potential problems you can run into when hosting your property through Airbnb. You've probably thought about items being broken or stolen and understand that you'll need to lock up valuables in a shared space or only provide decor that you aren't emotionally attached to. You've probably also considered the potential of toilets clogging, air conditioning or heaters malfunctioning, and power outages. But what are some other events you should be prepared to deal with?

Your personal liability as the property owner or contractually responsible tenant is one place to start. What would happen if a guest were to twist an ankle, fall down the stairs, or slip in the shower? Is it your fault? Do you owe them anything? What steps should you take through Airbnb to recognize the situation? Who needs to contact whom?

What if your guests should become violent or threaten you or someone who shares your home? What if they cause damage to a neighbor's property? Or, what if they simply refuse to leave, becoming a squatter on your property?

The guidelines for "who's responsible for what" aren't always cut and dry. Sometimes, local law and insurance guidelines supersede the presumed course of action. As an Airbnb host, you need to know who to contact, when to contact them, and what information both you and your guest will need to ensure that everyone is taken care of properly.

Chapter 1: Airbnb Policies Surrounding Safety and Security

Airbnb provides both hosts and guests with some resources to assist in maintaining safety and security throughout each stay. Whenever a listing or a booking is made through the site, all parties agree to Airbnb's terms and conditions. Granted, that's not a guarantee that everyone will behave in kind, but it does offer you some protection against foul play.

Your number one tool in dealing with any malicious guests is communication, starting with the very listing itself. Hosts are encouraged to create and post rules regarding their property and provide a clear and accurate description of the property within the post to prevent any issues up front. If the host clearly sets expectations prior to booking, then guests should have a good idea of what they'll encounter when they arrive.

Of course, they are also encouraged to ask questions of the host. Airbnb's primary recommendation for keeping everyone safe and secure is transparent communication. The site's policies ask hosts to respond to all communications as quickly as possible, but always within 24 hours. The downside is that much of the time devoted to communication may be fruitless work, as a hard-and-set pet policy, inaccessibility, parking difficulties, or other factors may prevent them from booking. On the other hand, having this discussion beforehand can prevent plenty of hurt feelings and anger in the future.

Once the booking is created, you'll continue to communicate with the guest before, during, and after their stay. At the bare minimum, you'll want to share check-in and check-out times, any access codes and send them a warm welcome before they arrive and gratitude after they depart. Most hosts enjoy checking in with guests throughout the stay to ensure expectations are being met.

Communication is the number one method for issue resolution before, during, and after the guests' stay. Guests and hosts alike are encouraged to contact each other if a minor problem arises, though Airbnb provides resources for conflict resolution if the situation escalates. Many issues are pretty simply dealt with, as long as both parties are calm, listening, and treating each other with respect. In fact, the majority of small problems can be resolved through excellent communication skills, preparedness, and patience on behalf of every party involved.

However, in the event that clear communication is ineffective or impossible, Airbnb does offer a Resolution Center tool. Through the app hosts are able to provide details directly to Airbnb staff to report wrongdoing or disagreements. This online tool helps walk through potential troubleshooting or allows hosts to connect with a representative for further assistance.

Airbnb also offers a robust extortion policy, which is part of the terms and conditions for site usage. Among the proscriptions within this policy, Airbnb does not permit the use of reviews – positive or negative – to threaten or elicit compensation from either hosts or guests. This means that if a guest has experienced any inconvenience, they are not permitted to leave a negative review if they didn't get their way. Similarly, the host is not allowed to leave negative reviews of guests unless their behavior truly was egregious. Furthermore, this prevents any potential sweeping of issues under the rug. Neither hosts nor guests can threaten each other with bad reviews in the event of a conflict.

This policy also applies to the incentivization of reviews. In the past, there were cases of hosts offering discounts or refunds for positive reviews, as well as guests threatening to leave false negative reviews if discounts or refunds are not received upon request. Paying the amount charged at the time of the booking is part of the deal, and all parties must adhere to this contract.

Additionally, Airbnb's policy regarding spam, phishing, and fraud is pretty straightforward. All parties are encouraged to complete financial transactions only within the site itself. Booking fraud (in which a "guest" books a stay using an invalid name, credit card number, or address), credit card fraud, cross-marketing, and money laundering are all strictly prohibited. Of course, Airbnb also considers abuse of the referral system and making false claims against guests or hosts to be violations of the site's terms of services.

In addition to restrictions, Airbnb provides specific protection to both hosts and guests to make the booking process as simple and secure as possible for everyone involved.

How Airbnb Protects Hosts

The most considerable risk that anyone takes when booking through Airbnb – whether they are the host or the guest – is that everyone involved is a stranger. While hotels offer a certain amount of security and established legitimacy, guests and hosts alike are bound to be wary about whom they may be cohabiting with or trusting in an unfamiliar space for a period of time.

Luckily, Airbnb has created a system to protect hosts from problematic or fraudulent bookings. While it would be impossible to predict an accident or an unruly guest, the site does take steps to ensure hosts are shielded from obvious problems.

First, each reservation is subject to Airbnb's risk scoring system. Using predictive analytics and algorithms, the site can discover suspicious activity and red flags that might not be abundantly apparent on the surface. Additionally, a background screening system is used to identify guests who may be on a regulatory or terrorist watch and checks sanctions and watchlists as well. In the United States, background checks are conducted by Airbnb for both hosts and guests.

Additionally, each person who uses the site must provide their full legal name, date of birth, phone number, email address, and valid payment information before they are able to book a space through the site. Hosts are permitted to request that guests verify a government ID through Airbnb's site before booking, as well.

As noted, before a booking is completed, guests are required to agree to your house rules. This means that hosts will need to be as abundantly clear as possible in setting expectations from the very first point of contact. In fact, if a guest uses the instant booking feature yet cannot agree to the house rules, a host can cancel the reservation through Airbnb without penalty.

While all of this is undoubtedly helpful, it cannot stop a guest from getting too drunk and destroying your bathroom. Unfortunately there's nothing that can prevent that scenario entirely. However, hosts can be as prepared as possible for dealing with that situation through the safety workshops Airbnb coordinates with local experts. Online support tools help arm hosts with possible solutions, tips, and pointers to help them through the process. Additionally, with so many other individuals turning to hosting as an exciting way to gain some income, it's not too difficult to network with other hosts who are happy to share some tricks of the trade.

Airbnb provides hosts with two distinct types of financial backing for unexpected situations: Host Protection Insurance and Host Guarantee. According to Airbnb's website, Host Protection Insurance can be used to provide coverage for:

- *Your legal responsibility for bodily injury to guests or others*
- *Your legal responsibility for damage to property belonging to guests or others*
- *Your legal responsibility for damage to common areas, like building lobbies and neighboring properties, caused by a guest or others*
  (https://www.airbnb.com/d/host-protection-insurance)

Conversely, it does not provide protection against loss of income, bodily injury or property damage caused by intentional acts, or damage caused to the host's home or personal belongings.

At its core, Host Protection Insurance is a type of liability insurance. The term "liability" refers to a property owner's financial responsibility when it comes to any accidental injuries or damages suffered that could be legally considered the homeowner's fault. For example, if a guest is descending a staircase and a step breaks, the host would be held responsible, or liable, for any medical care required as a result of the step breaking.

The determination of who is responsible for what gets hairier and more confusing depending on the situation, which makes it impossible to predict what kind of accidental damages a guest could encounter. Thankfully, insurance companies, including Airbnb's Host Protection, have clearly outlined definitions of what they will and will not cover.

Airbnb is willing to provide up to 1 million USD to pay for a host's liability in the event that a guest or third party should suffer an injury or property damage in conjunction with a stay at a property booked through Airbnb. In many cases, it acts as the primary insurance coverage. This means the host may not need to file a claim with their property and casualty insurance company. In addition, Airbnb provides online resources to help guide guests and hosts through filing a claim with Host Protection.

Separate coverage is offered for damages to a host's home or belongings: Airbnb's Host Guarantee. This is not considered a type of insurance but a property damage protection program that provides up to 1 million USD for damages incurred by the host due to a guest or guest's invitee during a stay.

As noted on Airbnb's website, Host Guarantee protection will cover:
- *Damage to your place caused by guests*
- *Damage to your belongings caused by guests*
- *Damage caused by a guest's assistance animal*
  (*https://www.airbnb.com/d/guarantee*)

Needless to say, it does not provide protection for natural wear and tear and will not cover theft of cash, stocks, or bonds. Again, hosts will document these situations and file a claim through Airbnb directly to request compensation through the Host Guarantee program.

As mentioned in the first section, these are types of policies and protections offered exclusively by Airbnb. Should you choose to host your property through another site or service, be sure to ask or research what types of insurance or safety measures they provide so you can avoid potentially dangerous situations and have coverage for any losses incurred.

While it is impossible to guess what kind of situations may arise while hosting travelers at your home or on your property, many hosts find peace of mind in knowing that insurance and other protections are available. These measures can mitigate huge expenses or jumps in insurance rates, depending on the circumstances. Again, be sure to consult with your personal insurance agent before you dive into hosting to ensure your coverage is appropriate for your hosting duties, and confirm how Airbnb's Host Protection and Host Guarantee programs coordinate with your property insurance.

How Airbnb Protects Guests

Airbnb also provides guests with certain security features and protection as well. Since it is required that all transactions occur online, all bookings are appropriately documented within the site.

This means that accounts and payments are recorded and handled through Airbnb. That way, Airbnb has a record of all payments, all refunds, all deposits, etc. This can be beneficial to both parties in the event that anything is contested; as we know, documentation is key when it comes to any type of conflict. The host should not have access to a guest's private account or payment information, which provides an extra layer of protection for guests on the off chance that something goes sideways.

Airbnb also encourages both hosts and guests to communicate strictly through the website or app's built-in messaging tool. There are two reasons for this. First, if something unfortunate were to happen, neither party would have the other person's private contact information. Secondly, this means that all communications between the parties would be on record through a single application. The "he said-she said" game can only last so long when there is only one recorded trail of interactions between the parties involved. This is part of what Airbnb terms a "multi-layer defense strategy" to prevent scams and minimize issue escalation.

Airbnb also provides guests with the ability to "flag" suspicious or inappropriate content at any time. Within each person's profile, listings, and direct messaging page, a flag icon will give users the ability to report anything that seems wrong.

Airbnb also wants guests to report any incidents that occur during a stay and provides a dedicated Trust and Safety team to field these situations. Guests are encouraged to first contact emergency services, including police, fire, or medical care, as appropriate for the situation. Then, once in a safe place and fully treated, guests are encouraged to report the situation through Airbnb's online channels.

Guests comfort and safety is also one of the main reasons hosts want to be sure that their listings are as detailed and accurate as possible. Guests are not only enabled to search for properties that can accommodate specific needs, but they are urged to thoroughly read each listing, host profile, and house rules in detail. If they don't find the details they need, it is recommended that travelers reach out to hosts directly via Airbnb's messaging system to ask questions.

In fact, Airbnb's Guest Refund Policy holds hosts accountable for the accuracy of the details provided in the listing for each property. If a guest books a stay and encounters what Airbnb deems a "Travel Issue" when they arrive on the property, they may qualify for a full or partial refund, depending on the timing and severity of the issue. "Travel Issues" are situations that arise due to hosts being untruthful, unreliable, or unclean, and per Airbnb's website, includes the following:

(a) the Host of the Accommodation
(i) cancels a booking shortly before the scheduled start of the booking, or
(ii) fails to provide the Guest with the reasonable ability to access the Accommodation (e.g. does not provide the keys and/or a security code).

(b) the Listing's description or depiction of the Accommodation is materially inaccurate with respect to:
(i) the size of the Accommodation (e.g., number and size of the bedroom, bathroom and/or kitchen or other rooms),
(ii) whether the booking for the Accommodation is for an entire home, private room or shared room, and whether another party, including the Host, is staying at the Accommodation during the booking,
(iii) special amenities or features represented in the Listing are not provided or do not function, such as decks, pools, hot tubs, bathrooms (toilet/shower/bathtub), kitchen (sink/stove/refrigerator or major other

appliances), and electrical, heating or air conditioning systems, or (iv) the physical location of the Accommodation (proximity).

(c) at the start of the Guest's booking, the Accommodation (i) is not generally clean and sanitary (including unclean bedding and/or bathroom towels) (ii) contains safety or health hazards that would be reasonably expected to adversely affect the Guest's stay at the Accommodation in Airbnb's judgment, or (iii) has vermin or contains pets not disclosed in the Listing.

(*https://www.airbnb.com/help/article/2868/airbnb-guest-refund-policy*)

Guests who encounter a Travel Issue must contact Airbnb directly via email, app, or telephone within 24 hours of uncovering the situation. Additionally, they must have "tangible evidence" of the issue, including photos, videos, or communications from the host that demonstrate the situation. Guests must also be willing to continue to communicate with Airbnb to facilitate a full investigation of the situation. Naturally, incidents caused directly or indirectly by the guest are not considered Travel Issues, which is why all parties are strongly encouraged to include and review as many details about each other and the property before agreeing upon a booking.

Hosts are required to include safety features on their property listings, and travelers are permitted to ask hosts questions to clarify these features. Airbnb hosts are offered a carbon monoxide monitor and smoke detector free of charge, which means these items should definitely be available for guests.

Guests are also guided to complete a safety check once they've arrived at a property. That includes making themselves familiar with entrances and exits, as well as safety equipment such as first aid kits and fire extinguishers. While this equipment may be an additional expense for hosts when starting out, having a comprehensive first aid kit and one or more fire extinguishers on hand can provide significant peace of mind for hosts and travelers alike.

Choosing to use the Airbnb platform as a host or a traveler includes a certain amount of inherent risk. In most cases, the parties involved are unfamiliar with each other, and the guest might be visiting a location for the first time. Naturally, reasonable people would carry a certain amount of apprehension about this scenario.

Airbnb is aware of the potential for scammers, untrustworthy people, and unavoidable accidents, which is why it offers several forms of protection for both hosts and guests. As a host, it is imperative to understand and appreciate the considerations that Airbnb has created for both parties. Hosts need to know what is expected of them, as well as the consequences for failure to deliver on those expectations.

Likewise, guests carry a certain burden of responsibility as well. They are required to fully investigate each property they are considering for a booking and choose only those that are appropriate for their requirements. When those requirements are not met, despite being promised, Airbnb provides avenues for guests to be refunded, just as hosts can be compensated for guests that do not hold up their end of the bargain.

Chapter 2: Support Team and Safety Equipment

The most common issues encountered by Airbnb hosts are relatively minor and can be fixed with quick attention and a healthy dose of patience. Clogged toilets, blown fuses, misbehaving HVAC units and the like are all common, everyday occurrences that anyone can sympathize with. These can usually be dealt with in short order, either by having the right equipment on hand or by contacting a specialist right away.

While a guest might be willing to plunge a toilet or reset a fuse on your circuit breaker, it's certainly not on their list of expectations while traveling.

Given that someone who has no idea what they're doing could potentially exacerbate the situation, you might be better off asking them to contact you directly.

This begs the question, who do you want your guests to contact in the event of a minor emergency and how do you want them to make contact?

If you plan to share your primary home with guests, obviously this is a simple process of knocking on your door or shouting urgently. But what if you don't share the home? What if you're not even close to the property?

Airbnb hosts accept that they'll need to be available around the clock when their property is booked for a stay. In most cases, contact with guests will be purely transactional– to settle check-in details, answer questions, and inquire about how things are going. However, what will you do if the power goes out at midnight in mid-winter and you're an hour away from the site? Or what if the water stops working while you're in the middle of a giant client presentation at the office? Obviously, you're not going to be glued to your cell phone or laptop to check Airbnb communications every moment, which means your guests could be left in a lurch.

One option to mitigate guest desperation and nasty reviews is to provide a list of emergency contacts. This list can include a host of helpful figures, including:

- A building supervisor or tenant relations manager
- A campground or site manager
- A maintenance expert or handyperson
- A plumber
- An electrician
- An HVAC specialist
- The internet/cable company

Granted, it may not be practical in all situations for your guests to contact these services directly. Some vendors refuse to deal with anyone but the homeowner or require a special security key to deal with inquiries. When you find vendors you can trust with these services, you may wish to inform them that your property is being rented through Airbnb. You might be able to set up a temporary security key that you can share with your guests for emergencies only or reach an agreement for specific scenarios.

You might also designate an emergency point of contact or a support team of your own. This can include friends or neighbors who are familiar enough with your property that they'll be able to do some basic troubleshooting. For example, if you have a heater that occasionally rattles when the settings aren't correct, this would be something your emergency contact would know and be able to address. Your support team can also include some acquaintances who have basic handy skills and necessary supplies, such as tarping a leaking roof, bringing heaters or fans if the HVAC system quits, or supplying water if the plumbing is off.

It is imperative to keep your Airbnb property in tip-top shape at all times, with regular preventative maintenance and inspections of all of your mechanical systems, utilities, pipes, and features. However, regardless of your attention to detail, things will go awry of their own accord, making preparation key.

This leads us to the topic of safety equipment. As mentioned earlier, smoke and carbon monoxide detectors are essential. First aid kits and fire extinguishers are also great assets to have on hand for any residents or visitors of your property. You never know when an ankle will twist, a finger will get cut, or a small flame will go out of control.

In addition to these common-sense items, you may wish to offer a few extra devices. This could include a plunger for the plumbing, batteries for the remote controls, flashlights, or fans and heaters stashed in a closet or utility room, as space permits. While you can't be prepared for every possible eventuality, you can be ready for common events, such as thunderstorms, clogged toilets, or blackouts.

Keep numbers for emergency services handy as well, including the fire, non-emergency police services, urgent care centers, or hospitals, depending on availability in your area.

In reading this chapter, it might feel like you're over-preparing. But bear in mind that even five-star hotels have emergency backup plans, including generators, evacuation plans, strategically placed fire hoses, sprinkler systems, and staff trained in first aid and CPR.

This is not to say that you have to have all of these options readily available. In fact, depending on the type of property you're renting, it might not make sense to have any or all of these. Where would you even install a carbon monoxide detector on a campsite, anyway? You will need to plan accordingly for the types of property and experience offered. People who have swimming pools will need to take safety precautions that those hosting stays in rustic cabins may never consider. When preparing, think from the standpoint of someone unfamiliar with your home and where they would turn in an emergency.

Chapter 3: Action to Take When Things Go Wrong

So, what should you do in the event of a true emergency or when a guest's actions become problematic?

One of the first recommendations of many seasoned Airbnb hosts is to document everything before, during, and after each stay.

Before your guests' check-in, preferably once you've completed the enhanced cleaning process, take pictures of everything. Many experienced hosts recommend taking pictures of every inch of your home, breaking rooms into sections to capture images of not just the furniture and decor, but also the current level of wear and tear on the space. From that tiny paint chip that's been there since the day you moved in, to the shining dust-free baseboards, it's a great idea to have baseline documentation of how things appeared before anyone showed up.

You may also wish to create a spreadsheet for your personal use, categorizing every item in your home. If you are furnishing a space that is not your own home, it's not a bad idea to hold onto receipts for each item in the space. Insurance companies typically have a standard rate they pay for damaged furniture, media devices, or decor unless you can provide them with proof of what it originally cost. In some cases, the expense may be nominal ("basket of flowers from garage sale: $2"), but what about bigger ticket items, like the bed, television, or appliances?

Doing this may seem an onerous process, but it can make a huge difference when attempting to prove to Airbnb and your insurance company that something is missing or damaged. So take your time, go room-by-room, and create a checklist of each item you have purposefully placed, where it is, a picture of it, and the retail price you paid for it.

You may only need to create the list once and use it as a checklist before and after each stay to ensure that everything is still present and in good condition. This list can also serve as a reminder to clean each object, too.

Before each guest's stay, you have the option to install security cameras. Airbnb's policies indicate that cameras in bathrooms or sleeping areas are forbidden, but they are permitted in outdoor spaces (such as entrances and exits) and in indoor common areas. Bear in mind that if you do have cameras installed, you need to specifically disclose this information on your listing. Cameras should also be highly visible so that guests are fully aware of when they are under surveillance.

The benefits of having constant video surveillance are many, especially if you do not live on the property full-time. Knowing who is coming and going from your property with cameras perched by the entrances, exits, and parking areas can give you peace of mind regardless of whether you've got an active booking. Today's technology also allows for simple integrated security systems, too, such as doorbells that record activity outside your home and home monitoring devices that can be accessed via a smartphone.

It's when you take the cameras indoors that you risk offending guests. Sure, if something does happen, you'd love to have that "fly on the wall" perspective to see how events unfolded. However, a majority of the time, you'll see guests wandering around your property, going about their everyday tasks. What if they like to enjoy their morning coffee au naturel or do morning yoga in the living room? Knowing they're being recorded could prevent them from fully enjoying the experience, and you might catch a glimpse of some perfectly natural moments that you might not want to see.

After your guests have checked out, you may wish to go over your property with a fine-tooth comb. If you live far away from the property, you may want to enlist the help of a buddy or assistant to take care of this process should the drive back and forth be too much to handle on a regular basis.

Your checklist can include as many details as you feel are prudent and manageable. From recording dents and dings to counting towels and silverware, from searching for stains to searching for things that might have snuck under the bed or lounging furniture, this is your time to make sure everything is right following a guest's stay.

This checklist can be incredibly beneficial for several reasons. First, you can correct any small incidentals, such as a minor scuff on a wall or a spill on the carpet that the guest attempted to clean up with whatever was on hand. The sooner you get to these unintentional damages, the easier they are to deal with. Second, if the guest has left any personal property at your home, you can reunite them with it faster. Children and pets are incredibly skilled at making toys and other small objects disappear. That means you could be the hero who reunited a child with her beloved stuffed animal, or you could solve the mystery of the missing spoons. Lastly, this allows you to create a comprehensive report to submit to Airbnb, rather than several contacts in which you keep adding or subtracting damages as you discover them.

The process for filing a claim with Airbnb is relatively straightforward. Whenever a host, guest, or third party contacts the site to report an incident, they will receive details on the claims process. The individual reporting the situation will be asked to complete an intake form, which is then reviewed by an adjuster assigned by Airbnb's insurance company. Typically, the adjuster will contact those involved to gain a full picture of the scenario, including the activity leading up to the claim and insight into what occurred. Claims are thoroughly investigated by the adjuster and settled according to Airbnb's regulation as well as any local laws or legal regulations in the host's area.

There are time limits on when a host can submit a request to the Resolution Center. If a host feels the security deposit would cover damages, the Resolution Center must be contacted before the next guest arrives or within 14 days, whichever happens first. If you have multiple back-to-back bookings, this means you need to act immediately.

Suppose the situation is not related to the security deposit. In that case, hosts may contact the Resolution Center to discuss the situation for up to 60 days following the guest in question's check-out date.

Airbnb is happy to step in and assist with disagreements between guests and hosts that are not reaching a conclusion. If a dispute has continued for more than 72 hours, hosts are encouraged to involve the Contact Center. At that point, a specialist will be assigned to your case, and they will be in touch to gather more information from each party involved. Once they feel they have gained enough insight into the root of the overall situation, they will provide their final decision on the matter.

As a host, you have a responsibility to yourself and to your guests to keep your property as safe and secure as possible. Unfortunately, there are likely to be a few bumps in the road throughout the process, especially as you're first getting started. Preventative maintenance and adequate safety equipment are a must. Communication is always your first line of defense, as many perceived issues can be worked out with a little patience and clarity. The likelihood of encountering a truly unpleasant situation or emergency is very small, but not zero. Therefore, before you begin actively hosting strangers in your home and on your property, it is crucial to have a sense of what could go wrong and what you will do to assist with and resolve the situation.

NOW WHAT?

You've made up your mind. You're going to go forth and become an Airbnb host. Whether you start acting on that right now, or slowly ease yourself into your upcoming venture, congratulations on making a huge decision!

So what can you expect, now that you're a part of the Airbnb community?

First, know that the bookings aren't going to be immediately and steadily streaming in. If you happen to list your property at a very convenient time, coinciding with vacation season or a huge event in your city, you might see a very quick and sudden flurry of activity. However, in most cases, you'll see a booking only once in a while for the first few months to a year of hosting.

This is not a bad thing. As you've read, becoming an Airbnb host isn't just an opportunity to make a little extra money; it can lead to really big lifestyle changes, especially if you plan to become a rental entrepreneur.

If you're feeling a little trepidation as you head into your first few bookings, feel free to have someone do a "dry run" with you. Choose someone you know to stay the night in your property and offer constructive feedback about what worked and what could use some attention. This is a great way to step outside of your own perspective to see what other people, who haven't spent months or years inside your four walls, think about your place. You can do this as many times as you need to get the feel for cleaning, setting up, walking through check-in and parking details, and so on. While it will likely take you more than a few visits to get everything feeling like routine, it's not a bad idea to physically walk through the process, instead of just running through it in your mind.

Remember also that those who are looking for a place to stay on Airbnb will be looking for affirmative reviews. They will know that you are new to this hosting gig. This is another place in which communication can help you tremendously. It's ok to explain that you are new to this, but you're excited to get started. Indicate that they can let you know if there's any way you can improve their experience. Most people understand that everyone has to start somewhere, and will provide you with plenty of positive feedback to help you with future bookings.

Another thing to consider is something called "Host Fatigue." This is a very real situation that nearly every host has experienced at some point. After a while, the whole process loses its enjoyable flair and becomes a chore. You find yourself irritated at answering the same questions over and over, especially when people would know the answers to those questions if they just read your listing in the first place! You're aggravated, irritable, and starting to question why you're doing this, anyway.

There are several steps you can take to prevent Host Fatigue, or overcoming it if it does settle in. First, if you're getting worked up about any less-than-five-star reviews, dig into what the source of the guests' frustrations are. Some guests don't fully understand the review system, believing it to be like a hotel star rating system. In their minds, three stars is great- it just means the property is more like a Red Roof Inn than a Plaza Hotel. As you read the actual review, it will be clear to you if this is the case, especially if the review has nothing but good things to say.

If the guest really did intend to leave a three or four star review based on their experience, take note. There will be opinions about things you can't change, such as street noise levels or inclement weather. Then there will be reviews that will dwell on something that was clearly mentioned in the listing, which they either didn't catch or chose to ignore. This type of review is an opportunity for you. How can you be more clear about this touch point? For direct critiques of your place, the furnishings, or the experience, don't immediately go on the defensive. Think about how you might incorporate the guest's feedback. Do you need to provide more direction or explanation? How can you do things differently? What can you add, delete, or change to make the experience different?

Another thing to consider is how you can interact with the guests differently. Some would benefit greatly from having a personal tour around the property or even a quick meeting over coffee to discuss their stay. This could be incorporated into the check-in process. You can be the judge of when these measures are appropriate, of course. If you have a single guest staying for just one night, they may not need to know about the neighborhood, but if you have a family checking in for two weeks, they'll definitely want to know the ropes.

If you prefer to stay hands-off, consider making an introduction video to send to guests at the time of the reservation. This could include a walkthrough of the property, along with where to find commonly requested household goods, like extra towels or utensils. Guests who watch these short, informal videos will feel even more confident with their booking. They'll have a visual that will help them feel as though they've already been to your place, even though they might not be arriving for weeks or months.

You may start to feel Host Fatigue after a long string of back-to-back bookings. Remember that you have the ability to block off time on your Airbnb listing, if you need a little rental vacation. You can also consider outsourcing your host duties to a trusted friend or one of your emergency contacts for a short period of time. Some features of Airbnb can be automated, depending on your hosting account and location, so feel free to take advantage of the options that are available to you. Despite the fact that you don't go to an office, this is a very real job, and as we've discussed, you'll be investing a lot of time and energy into preparation and cleaning. Don't be afraid to take time off for your own peace of mind.

Be flexible. Be willing to learn from your own experiences and others. Be interested in making changes that can benefit you and your guests. Your

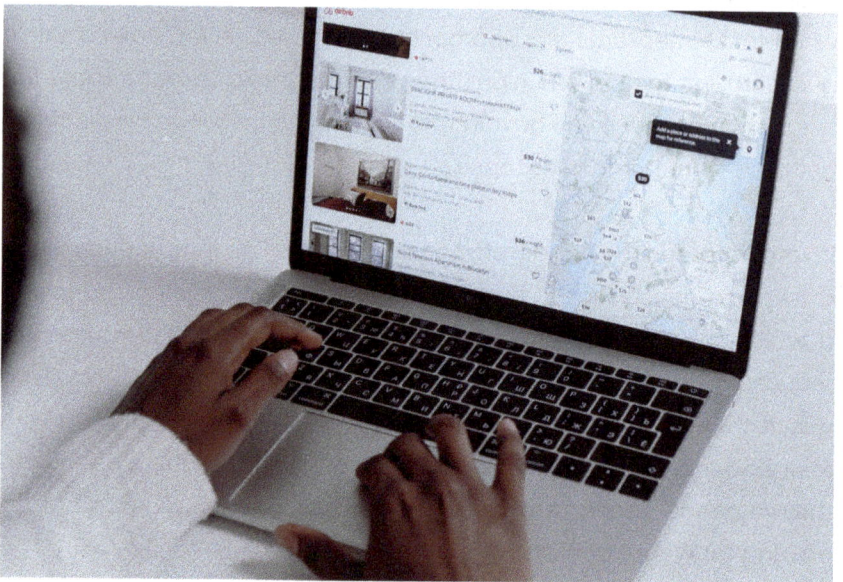

first few bookings may not go 100% according to plan, but with preparation, communication, and patience, you'll be able to navigate these uncharted waters safely, and make a little money too.

CONCLUSION

This book includes a lot of information to digest. Most of the information presented in these pages is based on common sense, and in some cases, the abundantly obvious. However, as a brand-new aspiring Airbnb host, how many of these concepts came to mind right away?

The goal of this book is to present a variety of considerations that hosts should have thought through before a guest books the very first stay at your property. Truthfully, even an amateur Airbnb host understands that the space has to be clean and ready to go. But your experience as a first-time host entirely depends on your own preparation. As yourself, would you rather have everything already in its place, with set procedures outlined and every detail clearly explained before the guest sets foot in your home... or would you like to find yourself scrambling for a spare roll of toilet paper at 3 am because you forgot to buy more?

Being prepared means better reviews and better reviews boost your listing's popularity. Regardless of whether your interest in becoming an Airbnb host is based on a simple desire to help out others, or if you have aspirations of becoming a big-time rental entrepreneur, you want positive reviews. No one likes to hear that their house is gross or that their interactions with the host were unilaterally unpleasant. Eventually, that sort of reputation will get a host banned from the site, making your investments of time, energy, and money all for naught.

You may have been surprised to discover what an investment starting your own Airbnb can be. It may very well be that having a spare space is the easiest part of the process! Unless you're renting a specifically rustic experience, such as a campsite, you will need to put some effort into your property. That means regular cleanings that bring your space up to Airbnb's specifically outlined requirements. That means extra maintenance to fix issues that might not be a problem to you but could cause trouble for anyone who doesn't know your property's unique quirks.

You'll also need to be able to look at your home objectively. Is this the kind of space where someone would really want to stay? Consider what might bring someone to your corner of the world. In some cases, a bed and a roof will suffice. In other situations, you're going to need to bring top-shelf luxury to attract regular clientele.

Business may start slow. Guests will look for reviews to validate whether or not your property is a good choice, and with very few (or none) to check, they may be wary at first. This is normal. In fact, a slow start gives you an extra opportunity to interface with guests to find out what they would like to see in your place, what is too much, and what could be changed.

You'll also need to do some juggling of priorities. Your home life, work hours, and any standing commitments you may have can interfere with your rising Airbnb business. What if you can't get to the property in time to check-in guests? What if you can't be available for emergencies during a particular period? You have many choices to make regarding your availability, your space, and assembling a support team who can step in when you are not nearby or accessible.

Now is a good time to check in with yourself. What were your feelings before you read these chapters? How do you feel now? What were some things that surprised you? What are some aspects of preparing your home that you're looking forward to, versus some things you might now be dreading?

You likely have some complex thoughts about hosting an Airbnb, and that's perfectly normal. One recommendation is to jot down these thoughts in a notebook, journal, etc. Just write down your thoughts as they come to you. Don't worry if they're repetitive or don't necessarily make sense in the context of clear literary language. Just write your thoughts. Once you've written out your most pressing thoughts, put the list away for a day or so. Then, once you're feeling more logical and less emotional, re-read your written thoughts.

Those that appear more than once are likely very important to you. You will want to carefully consider the thoughts that are pressing on your mind over and over again. For example, if you are in a remote location with a single spare bedroom and no neighbors, are you really going to be comfortable with a constant parade of strangers in and out of your home? If you have a hectic schedule, will you be able to remember to drop everything and get keys and parking passes to guests exactly at check-in time every single time? What if your guests don't share with you when they're planning to arrive? Can you sit around all day waiting for someone to knock on the door?

These are not questions with universal answers. In fact, for many of us, the answers to these questions can change from day to day. As an Airbnb host, you will need to be consistent and available or arrange a support team that can be there in your absence. Is that possible? Even more importantly, is that something you want to take on in your life?

Being a host for Airbnb (or any other room share or vacation rental program) can require a lot of you. A lot of time, a lot of patience, a lot of preparation, a lot of careful thought, and a lot of remembering a vast number of details.

You can always take it slowly and intentionally build your hosting program as you become more comfortable with what it takes. However, if you are feeling any serious trepidation or red flags now, pay attention to them. This is not something you have to do right away, nor do you need to rush to make all of the pieces fit when they might not otherwise work for you.

Every Airbnb host hopes to create a perfect experience for every guest, every time. That is simply not the reality. There will be unhappy guests. You will receive negative reviews for something out of your control. However, with the right level of insight, managing expectations, thorough preparation, patience, and clear communication, your overall Airbnb hosting career can be largely pleasant.

We wish you all the best with your Airbnb listing. Whether this is a dream come true, or a new adventure, hosting can be a deeply fulfilling experience with many great rewards. Best of luck to you and your listing!

RESOURCES

The following resources are intended to help summarize and provide clarity regarding the ins and outs of hosting through Airbnb. Many of the elements contained in the appendices will translate to any rental or home share company. However, it's always best to thoroughly read the rules and regulations of any business site before you move forward.

Additionally, bear in mind that things can change over time. These processes and regulations reflect publically available details at the time of publishing. It is possible for policies to be updated or altered in the future. Therefore, we ask that you not take these resources as a final word in the matter of Airbnb hosting, but rather as a starting point for your thoughts and considerations when turning your home into a place you would like to share with the public.

You may wish to print these resources, or create your own similar lists based on some adjunct thoughts you've had while reading this book. By all means, feel free to adapt these resources to your own needs and situation.

Becoming an Airbnb host should be a fun, educational experience for all. With all angles fully considered, you should feel a sense of clarity, confidence, and excitement as you step into this new business outlet. We wish you all the best, and may your guests be plentiful and pleasant!

Appendix A: Pros and Cons of Becoming an Airbnb Host

Pros	Cons
A wide selection of properties may be considered, including campsites, camper trailers, cabins, castles, room shares, tiny houses, houseboats, and more	It may not be legal in your area—you may need special permits or licenses (an extra expense)
Hosts set their own prices, which can change as needed	Your space or home must be in tip-top shape at all times
Airbnb does not charge a listing fee	You may need to buy extra furniture/decor
You can set your own calendar to only accept bookings during times that are convenient for you	You are responsible for cost of utilities offered to your guests, including water, electricity, gas, internet, and cable
Airbnb makes the process easy for you, from creating a listing, to providing blogs and videos that will walk you through various steps and questions	You will need to actively promote and market your property, respond to inquiries, and keep the pricing and calendar up to date
Payments and communications are arranged through Airbnb. You don't have to figure out how to process payments on your own	You will need to be available to respond to guest questions and requests 24/7
The opportunity to meet new people and make new friends can be wonderful—and can create frequent bookers	Added risk of accident, fire, flood, damage, or theft
You can earn 2-3x more renting your property through Airbnb than renting to a single tenant on a year lease	Added wear and tear to your property can lead to more frequent and costly maintenance
Airbnb offers protective measures to reduce risk to hosts	Bookings and income may be erratic or infrequent at first
The vast majority of guests are just looking for a nice place to sleep, creating minimum disruption for you	Added Airbnb service fees may be charged

Please note that this is not a comprehensive list, but it does relay the top ten pros and cons of Airbnb hosting, as reported by numerous hosts. Depending on your property and your goals, some of these items may not be relevant to your particular experience, or there may be greater considerations than are presented in this chart. Use this as a starting point to determine your own feelings and opinions on the topic of hosting, rather than viewing this as a definitive list of what to expect!

Appendix B: Are You Ready to Start Hosting? A Checklist

Here you'll find a list of things you need to keep in mind as you consider whether you're ready to become an Airbnb host. Essentially, this checklist summarizes many of the decisions discussed throughout the chapters of this book. This list is equal parts "things to remember" and "available options," which will hopefully get your own creative and logical juices flowing while you conceptualize your prospective Airbnb space. This list is in no way exhaustive, and the relevance of each item may wax or wane depending on the type of space you plan to share.

1: Your Home
- What about your home makes people want to stay there?
    - Location
    - Amenities/Extras (pool, hot tub, experiences)
    - Rare/Unique space
- What type of space will you provide?
    - Private Bedroom and shared space
    - Entire apartment
    - Entire condo
    - Entire cottage
    - Cabin
    - Castle
    - Houseboat
    - Tiny house
    - Campsite
    - RV

- Camper Trailer
- Other
- Where will your guests park?
  - Onsite
  - Shared parking space
  - On-street parking
  - Paid parking off-site
  - Other
- Who will share this space?
  - Roommates
  - Family
  - No one
  - Pets
  - Other
- Is this space appropriate for children?
  - All children/infants
  - Infants only
  - Older children only
  - Adults only
- Will you make your space available to pets?
  - All pets
  - Dogs only
  - Cats only
  - Caged pets only
  - None

2: Your Lifestyle

- How often can you rent out your property?
  - Every day
  - Every week
  - Every weekend
  - Once a month
  - Occasionally, as needed for extra income
  - Seasonally

- Where will you be while your space is occupied?
    - In my own home offsite
    - Sharing the space
    - Staying with a friend/family member/etc.
    - Undetermined, arrangements made as bookings come in
- How will you communicate with guests?
    - Through Airbnb only
    - In person
    - Via text or phone call
- Can you be available 24/7 for guests' needs?
    - Yes
    - No, but I'll designate a support team/emergency contact for each booking
    - No, but I'll share my limited availability with each guest
- What will you do with your personal property while your space is in use?
    - I don't live onsite and have no personal property at the location
    - No personal property will be displayed or available in common areas
    - I'll lock it up during the busy seasons
    - I'll take my chances

3: Cleaning and Staging
- Can you adhere to Airbnb's enhanced cleaning process?
    - Yes, I'll take care of the cleaning myself
    - Yes, but only if I hire a cleaning company
    - Yes, but it will take me a while and limit my ability to accommodate back-to-back bookings
- What will you need to clean and stage the following spaces:
    - Bedroom
        - Vacuum
        - Laundry

- Dust
- Disinfect
- Examine beds and bedding for stains
- Look in each drawer and under all furniture for items left behind
- Air out the room
- Bathroom
  - Clean and disinfect all surfaces
  - Toilet
  - Sink
  - Bathtub/shower
  - Floor
  - Countertops
  - Restock toiletries
    - Provide extra toilet paper/tissues
    - Keep an adequate stock of soap/shampoo on hand at all times
  - Launder towels- recommended two sets of towels per guest
  - Launder bath mats/rugs
  - Ensure toilet/sink/shower/bath are all in working order
  - Change shower curtains frequently
  - Eliminate mold and rust stains
  - Provide, empty, and clean trash cans
- Kitchen
  - Clean and disinfect surfaces
  - Do dishes/run dishwasher
  - Clean and disinfect appliances
    - Oven
    - Stovetop
    - Refrigerator shelves
    - Freezer
  - Clean floors

- Clean rugs or mats
- Make sure all appliances and fixtures are working
- Check supply of cookware, serveware, utensils, and cups
    - Are any broken?
    - Are any missing?
    - Do you have enough available for the next reservation?
- If snacks or coffee are provided, clean area and restock
    - Snacks
    - Coffee filters
    - Coffee
    - Creamer
    - Sugar/Sweeteners
    - Stir sticks
    - Coffee cups
- Run garbage disposal
- Remove all trash and recycling
- Restock bin liners, dish soap, cooking implements, and basic cleaning products
- Living areas
    - Clean and disinfect all surfaces
    - Vacuum and steam/mop floors
    - Inspect all furniture for stains and spot clean
    - Inspect all furniture for signs of wear and tear or damage
    - Make sure batteries in remote controls are working
    - Check light bulbs in lamps
    - Check pillows/blankets/accessories for stains, wear and tear, or damage
    - Launder pillows/blankets/accessories as appropriate

- Outdoor living areas
    - Ensure railings and flooring are safe and clean
    - Inspect and clean features such as grills, hot tubs, pools, etc.
    - Inspect furniture for stains, wear and tear, or damage
    - Check for potential maintenance issues
- General
    - Check floors, walls, ceilings, closets for potential damage and forgotten items
    - Take inventory of all objects that are accessible to guests before and after each stay. If anything is lost, broken or destroyed, be sure to replace it as applicable.
    - Encourage good behavior by labeling, providing adequate trash and cleaning supplies, and posting requests and reminders where they can be easily viewed by guests.

4: Extras
- Determine what you will provide for your guests. Some options include:
    - Bathroom
        - Soap
        - Shampoo
        - Conditioner
        - Body wash
        - Makeup removal towels
        - Menstrual products
        - Hair dryer
    - Bedroom
        - Extra blankets
        - Extra pillows
        - Heaters

- Fans
- Dehumidifiers/Humidifiers
- Power strips
- Laundry detergent
- Kitchen
  - Sponges/dish cloth
  - Dish detergent
  - Pots/pans/cookware
  - Utensils
  - Cooking oil and spices/seasoning
  - Ice
  - Drinking water
  - Glasses/cups
  - Coffee supplies
  - Teabags
  - Tea kettle/electric kettle
  - Small appliances (toaster, electric griddle, blender, etc)
- Living area
  - Pillows
  - Blankets
  - Lamps
  - Television
  - DVD player
  - Streaming television capability
  - WiFi

  - Coasters
  - Power strips
  - TV Trays
  - Games/Puzzles
  - Books
- General
  - First aid kit

- Fire extinguisher
- Carbon monoxide detector
- Smoke detector
- Security system
- Fans
- Heaters
- Coat rack/storage space
- Shoe tray
- Umbrellas

5: Parking and Transportation
- Where do guests park?
- What type of pass or device do they need?
- What does off-site parking cost, if applicable?
- Does your area have public transit?
  - Provide a map or directions to nearest stop
- Are taxis or rideshares available?
- Are there restrictions surrounding on-street parking spaces?

6: Check-in/Check-out
- Will you be present to meet and greet guests?
- Do guests need a key?
- Will you provide a lockbox/security system/entry code for remote check-in if you will not be present?
- If check-in is remote, do you want guests to alert you when they have arrived?
- What time is check-in/check-out?
- How do guests return their keys to you?
- Do you want guests to notify you when they vacate the property?
- Will you allow for luggage drop off if guests arrive early or need to park off-site?

7: Communication
- Rules and regulations

- How will you share house rules with your guests?
- Will you create a house manual?
- Will you label cabinets and drawers?
- Will you post specific rules throughout the house (eg: "Do not set the thermostat below 62⬚." "Unplug chargers when you leave the house." "Be sure to turn off the coffee maker.")

- Preferred communication methods
  - How do you prefer guests to contact you for general inquiries?
  - How do you want guests to contact you in an emergency?
  - Will you provide emergency contact numbers?
  - How will you share this contact information, if it's a method other than Airbnb messaging platform
- Emergency Contacts/Support Team
  - Will guests be permitted to contact service vendors in an emergency?
  - Do you prefer guests to contact you before or after they attempt to deal with an emergency?
  - Which member of your support team will be available in which circumstances? (eg: time of day, type of situation)

8: Are You Ready?
- Do you have the time to invest in getting things going?
- Are you comfortable with having strangers in your home?
- How do you think the unpredictable nature of hosting will make you feel?
- Do you consider yourself organized?
- Do you have a flexible schedule?
- Are you ok with answering phone calls and emails at any time of day?
- Do you have the money and time to get your property cleaned and staged between each stay?
- How frequently are you going to make your property available?

- What do you want to get out of this experience?

Appendix C: Airbnb Administrative Processes

Once you're all set and ready to begin hosting, it's time to start the administrative processes. This means creating an account, building your profile, and adding your listing. To get started, you'll need to block off time to sit down and think about how to best market yourself and your property. You'll need clear photographs of every room available to your guests. You'll want to have a concept of what you plan to offer and how you plan to provide it. And, practically speaking, you'll want to have a well-behaved laptop, phone, or device with a solid internet connection.
Creating an Account

The very first step is to create an account with Airbnb. This means creating a username and password, of course, but you'll also need to create your user profile.

An ideal user profile will include a minimum of fifty words and a picture of yourself. The goal of this is to create a sense of credibility and to start introductions off right away. Remember that you and your guests will likely be complete strangers. However, if they have the opportunity to see your face and learn a few things about who you are, that will make you less unfamiliar with each other and lend authenticity to the situation. You might even be able to bond over some common ground. Your profile does not need to include your entire biography. Instead, you want to provide some insight into your personality. For example, you might mention your favorite band, or things you enjoy doing in your town or city. You can even share why you've decided to become a host.

You also have the option of verifying your identity through Airbnb. This usually involves uploading a picture of your government ID to the site. This information is never shared with guests; in fact, they'll receive only your first name and whether you're over or under 25. Your phone number and the property address aren't released until a booking has been made and authenticated! You can also request that guests are authenticated as well, through the same process.

Your Listing

Next, it's time to create the listing itself. Creating your listing goes much further than indicating how many bedrooms and bathrooms there are. You want to paint an accurate picture of your property.

Start with the name of the listing. Most hosts use the type of property and location. Examples include: "Entire Cottage - Waterfront - Lake Superior." "Entire Guest Suite - Georgetown." "Private Room - Castle - Ireland." These are the types of things that will intrigue a traveler and encourage them to drill down and learn more.

One trick some hosts recommend is to sit down with a friend and take turns describing your property to each other. Everyone will view your space in a slightly different way, so getting some insight into how others appreciate it can help you create an accurate representation of each room.

Take time to focus on the things that make your place unique. This is where the amenities and extras will really make a difference. You don't have to provide a detailed description of how comfortable the sofa is or the thread count in your sheets, but if you have something fun like floor-to-ceiling windows or a hot tub, mention it. Doing this can give you an advantage over other listings in your area.

You'll also want to be abundantly clear in your listing about any other inhabitants, such as roommates, but especially pets. Any potential allergens should also be addressed in the initial listing.

Start with an "all about my place" description. This might sound a little like a real estate listing, but that's ok. You're painting a picture of the space. Mention things like hardwood floors, lots of natural light, open floor plans, or skylights. Then be sure to share how much space guests will have. Is it an entire condo? A single bedroom and a bathroom? A detached bathroom? These are all details guests want to know.

What appliances will they have access to? Refrigerator? Stove? Microwave? Coffee maker? High-speed internet? List all of these things out as well. Then make a few brief notes about special considerations: "Accessing the apartment requires two flights of stairs." "Ground floor entrance." "Wheelchair accessible ramp in the rear." You may also wish to share the location of a fire extinguisher and first aid kit, or confirm whether smoke and carbon monoxide detectors are present.

Next is your list of amenities. For the sake of an Airbnb listing, this can include everything from hot water and clothes hangers to free shampoo and cooking implements. Be honest here, and be consistent with what you promise. If you note that you are providing towels and linens, be sure to have a surplus of clean towels in good condition awaiting your guests when they arrive.

House rules can also be posted in your listing. You may not need to get too in-depth with your requirements, but here is a great place to post check-in and check-out times, whether your home is appropriate for pets and children, and rules about smoking, candles, and parties. Remember, your guests will receive an electronic copy of your regulations once they request a booking with an acknowledgment that by proceeding with their booking they are agreeing to all of the provided rules.

Don't forget that photographs are a huge part of the listing. Take pictures of the inside and outside of your property (as applicable) so that guests are able to recognize where they are going and get a feel for the layout of your home. If you have a particularly fascinating layout, you may wish to post a rudimentary floor plan to your listing as well. Highlight important features such as the bedroom(s), kitchen, and bathroom(s) so that guests are fully aware of what to expect.

Marketing

One of the benefits of hosting through a site like Airbnb is that you don't have to do very much external marketing. You don't have to start a website or develop a social media presence to get traction on your location. You don't need to create content, link exciting articles, or any of the popular online business marketing tricks that so many companies use today. Airbnb takes care of the marketing for you. All guests need to do to find your property is search in your location, for a date range in which your property is available, or for certain features included in your home. If they're looking, Airbnb will help them connect with you via their search system. That's not to say you can't market your property separately, but more on that in just a moment.

However, there are still some ways to make your listing stand out from the rest of the list. The first is through the photos you use. Hotels and real estate ads post clean, crisp, well-lit photos of their properties to attract more viewers, and so should you. Airbnb does offer hosts access to a professional photography service for many locations. You can request professional photos through the site, and the cost of the session will be deducted from your future bookings. This means you don't need to shop around for photographers who have experience shooting homes and interior spaces, though you are certainly welcome to do so.

If you choose to take and post your own pictures, there are a few things to keep in mind. First, you'll want to make sure the room is completely clean and presentable. This shouldn't be difficult, since you're preparing to have strangers stay in this space, but it never hurts to run an extra glance over every inch of the space. Something like a wrinkle in a towel or a pillow that has slumped over will draw the viewer's eye and disturb the entire shot.

Next, pay attention to lighting. If at all possible, take pictures on a sunny day. Turn on all the lights. While your guests may not ever turn on all the lights at once, everything looks darker in photos. Make sure they can see every detail of the room, and that there aren't any harsh shadows blocking important features like the bed or parts of the kitchen.

You may need to bring in some lights from other rooms, or have a friend hold a light ring as you take photos. While this may seem like the most straightforward part of creating your listing, you still want to take your time and do a good job. You don't want guests squinting at your pictures saying, "what *is* that?" You want them to see the space as it honestly appears, with the features they will be able to access when they arrive.

Outdoor pictures are also important. Guests want to be able to recognize where they're staying when they first arrive. As you can imagine, they're already feeling a little anxious about spending the night in a strange place. Help them feel welcome by providing a shot of the front door to your home or your building, so they know they're in the right spot and feel confident walking through that door.

When uploading your photos, make sure you do so in an order that mimics the flow of the house. Start with the front door, then move to the foyer, and so forth. Give viewers a feel for the footprint of the space, and take them on a tour of the space, rather than giving them a series of photos in no particular order.

You may wish to share pictures of your property during various seasons, too. This can be especially important for rustic or rural listings, where the beauty of nature comes alive during particular seasons.

You want the pictures that accompany your listing to tell a story, but don't be afraid to actually tell a story in your listing, as well. Add captions to your photos. Included plenty of details in your listing, as well. Sure, your photos should speak for themselves, but there are certain things you just can't capture in a picture. For example, your high thread-count sheet set probably doesn't look different from other sheets in a basic photograph.

No one can tell how comfortable your bed is from photos. Things like surround sound, heated tiles, massaging shower jets and the like simply don't translate well into photos, but you can certainly describe them.

You don't have to be a professional writer to create a compelling listing, but be sure to give your description some flavor. Channel some of your own excitement for the property into the listing. For example, you can invite viewers to "watch the sunrise from the east-facing kitchen window while sipping complimentary coffee" rather than saying "coffee is in the kitchen for your use."

Make sure you proof-read your article, too. Typos happen, but depending on what autocorrect or a slip of the finger does, you can confuse your audience very quickly. Read and re-read your posting before you submit it, and check it in full each time you make any adjustments to your listing (such as calendar updates or price changes).

Regarding your own marketing strategy, you can choose to do a little external work to drum up excitement about your space. Social media is one way to share your new journey. Instagram is a very popular site for Airbnb hosts to share photos of their property along with news about their location, or fun events coming up. Naturally, this is not necessary for casual renters, but if you are looking to become a rental entrepreneur, you'll want to give your property as much exposure as possible.

Some Airbnb hosts connect with local social media influencers and offer collaborations. The influencer can enjoy a discounted stay, as long as they share how amazing the experience was via their blog, vlog, or social media channels. Hosts may also wish to run contests or giveaways via their personal social media accounts, or hold events in the space when it's not booked. Hosting an event may not seem related to social media until you start seeing your location or hashtag trending, which will bring you more hits and prospective customers.

You'll also want to stay close to the community. Whether that's the campground staff for the RV you're renting to guests, the cafes and restaurants closest to your home, or even the kind folks at the only gas station around for 20 miles, networking within your community will help your guests have an even better time while at your property. Whether they're looking for directions back to the place or asking for more recommendations about the area, it helps if the proprietor knows who you are and the general vicinity of where your Airbnb is located. In a huge city, this might be impossible, but introducing yourself to the staff at the corner shop underneath your apartment and explaining you run an Airbnb could work out in your favor in the long run.

While heavy marketing may not be your top priority in establishing yourself as an Airbnb host, there are certainly measures you can take that help you stand out from the rest of the listings in your area. At first, this will help gain new bookings, which will lead to more reviews. More positive reviews will encourage more guests to book your space, and your business will continue to grow from there. Just remember to tell your story in pictures and words the best you can to attract potential guests from around the world to choose your listing over others.

Pricing

Pricing is perhaps the most challenging part of the process, as it can be somewhat arbitrary and subject to change, depending on seasonality and local events. The good news is that you can change your pricing as needed.

If your goal as an Airbnb host is to one day become a rental entrepreneur, you'll need to pay attention to market values in your area on a near-constant basis. What do local hotel rooms charge? What kind of amenities and extras do they provide? What about your home has added value over the local motel? What about other Airbnb listings in your area? How do prices increase or decrease seasonally? How much do other hotels or rental properties increase their prices during certain community events?

To be competitive, you need to keep up with the competition. It seems obvious, but that may mean spending hours in front of the computer doing research and reading listing after listing for local hotels, motels, bed and breakfasts, and other Airbnb listings. When a local event spikes interest in your area, you will want to monitor local pricing so you can gain the highest level of profit without pricing yourself out of the market altogether. You may wish to amp up the offerings inside your home during these "peak" periods to gain the highest number of bookings at the highest price.

If you are casually or infrequently providing a place for others to stay, you might take a "set it and forget it" approach to your pricing. Still, you need to make sure that what you charge aligns with what you offer. If you price yourself too low, you may draw suspicion from potential bookers. Alternately, you might find yourself inundated with endless bookings from people who love a good deal.

Do the math to ensure that what you charge is worth the effort and expense. Add up your typical utility costs, cost of supplies, laundry, linens, upkeep etc. Any dollar you put into your Airbnb listing should be reflected in the price you charge your guests. Make sure you don't price yourself out of a sustainable business. All that toilet paper, complimentary soap, cleaning between bookings, and laundry can add up to a lot of extra time and money.

At least once a week, take a look at other listings in your area to make sure you're on target for your goals and location. Doing this will help you keep your pricing reasonable and competitive at all times.

Reviews

The reputation of both guests and hosts on Airbnb is gauged by reviews. Hosts may provide reviews for guests, and guests may provide reviews for hosts. These are publicly displayed on each listing and profile, so anyone searching for the perfect place can see for themselves if it is a good fit.

Guests can only leave reviews after they have checked out, which means the reviews will be based on actual experiences. Hosts are encouraged to read and respond to these reviews, as well, but remember to always keep a professional tone. Yes, your guests may plainly demonstrate that they did not read your description or rules, but this is your opportunity to reiterate those facts. Be kind, and leave the drama for the Airbnb Contact Team when you're working through resolutions. These reviews are public, and some potential guests may not want to engage with a host who appears irritable or defensive.

The same goes for leaving reviews for your guests. You don't need to go into deep detail. Instead, comment on what went well. Did they leave the place tidy? Were they quiet and respectful? How was the communication? Be honest, of course, but this is not the time to air any "dirty laundry." The point of hosts reviewing guests is so that future hosts will know what to expect from a guest. A laundry list of all the things you liked and didn't like about them is entirely unnecessary.

The most important thing to keep in mind about reviews is that both parties have the opportunity to write both a public and private review. The public reviews will help other hosts and guests form an opinion about your listing and you as a host. When you're creating your Airbnb experience, keep this in mind, and aim to construct a setting and ambiance that will reach for the stars... that is, five-star ratings. For everything you do, do it for the guest's comfort and happiness, and that will translate into higher ratings and glowing reviews.

Additionally, be sure to check out Airbnb's online host resources. There are plenty of videos, blogs, and articles that can help you navigate the administrative processes when you're just getting started. These resources can help inspire and inform you, as well as give you new things to think about when marketing your property. Plus, this will provide you with immediate insight into any procedural changes and updates.

REVIEWS

Reviews and feedback help improve this book and the author. If you enjoy this book, we would greatly appreciate it if you could take a few moments to share your opinion and post a review on Amazon.